THE GHOST IN THE GALLERY

A ghostly figure, a walking suit of armor, and a gargoyle in the prompter's box confront Jean and Louise Dana and their Starhurst classmates as they rehearse for a musical at the Mozart Hall. The owner, a retired singer, and the watchman assure the performers there is nothing to worry about. The students wonder whether their imaginations are playing tricks on them. Or are spooky things actually happening each time they visit the opera house?

A contest is held for an original song to be used in the play. The Danas' music is stolen but they make a copy and submit it. When their song is chosen as one of the winners, a listener says she has heard it before!

Louise and Jean face danger and intrigue, but they work hard to solve several mysteries and to win out over their enemies.

The suit of armor was moving slowly across the floor!

The *Dana Girls* Mystery Stories

THE GHOST
IN
THE GALLERY

By Carolyn Keene

GROSSET & DUNLAP

Publishers   *New York*

CONTENTS

THE GHOST
IN THE
GALLERY

CHAPTER I

Missing!

"LOUISE Dana! You startled me in that Louis XIV costume. For a second I thought you were a boy!"

Professor Crandall had stopped in the hallway of the Starhurst School for Girls to speak to Louise and her sister Jean. There was a twinkle in his blue eyes as he stared at attractive, dark-haired seventeen-year-old Louise. Then he turned toward Jean, pretty and blond. She was a year younger than Louise and slightly shorter. Over one arm she carried a velvet-and-lace dress.

Both girls laughed merrily at the elderly professor's mistake. He taught history at Starhurst and was the husband of the school's headmistress. The professor was a good-natured man but inclined to be absent-minded at times.

"We're both going to be in the show," Louise explained. "It's an original mystery musical."

"Musical?" the professor echoed, puzzled, but

immediately said, "Oh, yes, I remember. And you will be in costume, too?" he asked Jean.

"I'm to be a young woman of the Louis XIV period."

As the professor asked other questions, the sisters could hardly stifle their giggles. He could recall very little about the plans for the show, although it had been the main topic of conversation throughout the school for a month.

The girls reminded him that the musical was set in the Louis XIV period and was called *Spring Is Here*. Students at the boarding school had been asked to submit original songs for the play.

"Louise and I have written one," Jean told him. "We hope we'll be lucky and that ours will be among the final four chosen."

Professor Crandall smiled. "I wish all four of you luck," he said, and turned into his office.

Louise and Jean were still laughing as they went upstairs to their two-room suite. They slept in one room and used the other as a study.

"Let's take our song over to Miss Rosemont," Louise suggested. She was the head of the Music Department. "We'll just have time to change our clothes and get back to dinner."

Jean agreed and the girls hurriedly donned pastel summer dresses. Then Louise opened her desk drawer to take out the sheets of music.

"Our original song is gone!" she exclaimed.

Louise thoroughly searched her desk, then Jean went through hers. Next, they looked in their bureau and night-table drawers, and finally under the beds.

"You don't suppose that new maid, Fritzi Brunner, threw it away by mistake?" Louise asked.

"We can soon find out," Jean said. "Come on!"

The sisters hurried to the school employees' dining room, where the maids were having dinner. When the Danas asked about the music, Fritzi declared she had not seen it.

More concerned than ever over the loss of their song, Jean and Louise left the room. In the hall Fritzi caught up with them.

"Please," she said, half-whispering, "tell me how you go about finding lost articles. I heard that you girls are detectives."

The Danas said they had solved a few mysteries. They promised to give Fritzi some pointers on tracing missing items, but at present there was not enough time.

Back in their room, Jean said with determination, "There's one place I'm going to start searching right now."

Louise smiled. "I can see by the look in your eyes that you suspect Lettie and Ina of another mean joke."

"You're right. This whole thing is exactly their idea of something funny."

"Our original song is gone!" Jean exclaimed.

Lettie Briggs was an unpleasant girl. Intensely jealous of Louise and Jean's popularity, Lettie did everything possible to make trouble for them.

Ina Mason was her roommate, and while she never thought up anything original, she played a part in all of Lettie's schemes. The two girls were not in their room, and the Danas' original song was not in sight.

"I wish we dared go through their bureau and desk drawers," said Jean. "Lettie and Ina might have tucked it away underneath something."

"If Lettie is to blame, she'll probably give herself away," Louise commented. "We'd better hurry or we'll be late for dinner."

The two girls she suspected were seated directly opposite the sisters at one of the large round tables in the dining room. During the meal, neither Lettie nor Ina showed any sign of guilt.

Presently Mrs. Crandall rose to make an announcement. A tall, slender woman whom the students both liked and feared, she was a strict disciplinarian but fair in her judgments.

"I thought you would be interested to know that plans for our musical are progressing most satisfactorily," the headmistress said. "Townspeople are showing great interest in it, and I have had letters from many parents who plan to come."

She smiled. "I must confess that I did not realize the musical would be so popular. We have sold more tickets than the capacity of our school auditorium. It is unfortunate, but I am afraid we shall have to disappoint anyone else who may wish to attend *Spring Is Here*."

There were groans from several sections of the dining room. Louise said quietly to Jean, "We haven't bought tickets for Uncle Ned and Aunt Harriet yet!"

Miss Harriet Dana and Captain Ned Dana were brother and sister. Louise and Jean, who had been orphaned when they were three and four years old, had lived with them since then. Their uncle, who was captain of an ocean liner, the *Balaska*, was away a great deal of the time, but expected to have a short vacation during the week of the musical.

"They'll be terribly disappointed if they can't see us in the show." Jean sighed. Suddenly an idea came to her and she stood up. "Mrs. Crandall, perhaps we could rent Mozart Hall."

The theater was an old unused opera house in the center of Penfield. Years before, it had been a popular spot. But when traveling opera companies had ceased to come to the town, the theater had been closed.

Recently it had been bought by Mrs. Mulford Merrill, a former opera singer who lived in a rambling, old-fashioned house next door to Mozart Hall. She was a wealthy, charitable person, and had purchased the opera house for sentimental reasons. Many years before, at the peak of her career, the singer had often performed there.

"I think your suggestion is a very good one, Jean," Mrs. Crandall said. "The more tickets we can sell, the more money we will be able to give to the Penfield charities. I'll speak to Mrs. Merrill about renting the building to us. And now I'll say good evening."

When Louise and Jean returned to their room, they resumed the search for the missing song, but finally gave up and sat down at their desks to make another copy. Across the top of a fresh sheet of paper Louise printed the title, "We're All Mysterious."

Jean started to hum the tune, but Louise gave a warning sh! "Remember, it's supposed to be a secret," she said.

At breakfast the following morning Mrs. Crandall announced with delight that she had made arrangements with Mrs. Merrill to hold the performance of *Spring Is Here* in old Mozart Hall.

"Mrs. Merrill has been most generous," the headmistress said. "She is lending the building to us. But she has warned——" Mrs. Crandall paused, then resumed. "Mrs. Merrill has warned us that it is said the old opera house is haunted. Of course there is nothing to this story and I don't want any of you girls to become nervous during rehearsals."

Mrs. Crandall sat down and Jean laughingly remarked, "I just can't wait to see what's haunting the old opera house!"

Lettie Briggs gave her a disdainful look. "Aren't you the brave one!" she said sourly. "You may change your mind if that broken-down place is full of spooks."

After classes that afternoon, Louise and Jean were summoned to the headmistress's office. Mrs. Crandall said she had obtained a key to Mozart Hall and had looked over the place. Although old, the building was perfectly safe.

"I thought perhaps you girls would like to take some of your friends there and see what it's like," she suggested. "Since using Mozart Hall was your idea, Jean, I'm giving you the key. Probably there'll be a good bit of cleaning to do before we can hold rehearsals there. Suppose you report to me on what work will be required."

The sisters, thrilled with the assignment, immediately hurried off to round up some of their friends. First they asked Evelyn Starr, whose family had owned Starhurst estate before it became a school. She was a very attractive girl and the Danas' best friend.

They also found that Doris Harland, Ann Freeman, and Margaret Glenn were not busy and were eager to go along. The six girls started at once for Mozart Hall, which was located on the main street about halfway between the school and the center of town.

Jean unlocked the huge, creaky front door and led the way inside. Since the electricity in the building was off, the girls had brought flashlights. They turned them on, then crossed the lobby and went into the auditorium.

The silence of the vast room was almost overpowering. The girls tensed a little as they cautiously headed for the stage.

An eerie cry from the rear stopped them abruptly. Everyone turned. Up in the third gallery stood a figure sheathed in white, a weird light playing around it.

"A g-ghost!" Doris shrieked.

CHAPTER II

Startling Figures

As Doris Harland's scream echoed through the opera house, the weird, bluish-white light around the ghostly figure vanished. The group of girls, their pulses racing, stood in silence as they stared up at the dark third gallery.

Finally Louise found her voice. "Was I seeing things?" she asked slowly.

"You certainly weren't," replied Doris, who was still shaking with fright. "There was a ghost up there and no mistake about it."

Suddenly Jean began to laugh. "If you ask me, this is one of Lettie's tricks."

Evelyn remarked that she was not sure it was a trick. She vaguely recalled having heard a story in connection with the opera house that might account for the mysterious episode, but she could not remember it.

The girls returned to the lobby, then started

up the broad stairway marked TO THE THIRD
GALLERY. Its threadbare red carpet was mute evidence of the former grandeur of Mozart Hall.

When they reached the top, the searchers
beamed their lights along the corridor and across
the semicircular area of seats. No one.

"There must be a secret exit," Louise suggested,
but they could find none.

"That means," Doris insisted, "there really was
a ghost here. I vote we go back to school at once!"

"And not accomplish what we came to do?"
Louise asked. "This would be a wonderful place
for us to give the musical and I want to look all
around—ghosts or no ghosts!"

All but Doris agreed that this was the only
sensible thing to do.

"If we stick close together," Margaret said,
"nothing can happen to any of us."

The group walked down to the lobby, then
went up a stairway that led to the first and second
galleries. These were more formal and ornate than
the third balcony. The boxes of the first tier were
curtained off with heavy plush portières.

Louise drew one aside and gasped. Inside stood
the shadowy shape of a woman in a Spanish costume.

"Oh!" Louise exclaimed. "For a second I
thought she was real!"

As the others crowded into the box, Louise

beamed her light directly on the human-sized form.

"The señorita certainly looks lifelike," Jean admitted.

The girls continued their inspection of Mozart Hall and came across many more figures. Some were lovely white marble statues; others, dummies dressed in costumes from various operas.

Finally the group reached the vast stage. Ann Freeman flashed her light upward and said, "What a complicated set of gadgets!"

The others were intrigued too by the many ropes and pulleys that went up the back wall of the stage and across the very high ceiling all the way to the front. There were ladders to three fly galleries: one on each side of the stage and one running directly across the center of the ceiling.

As the Danas and their friends wondered how the various gadgets and apparatus were used, an unfamiliar voice said, "Good afternoon, girls!"

Everyone whirled. From one of the wings stepped a tall, stately woman. She was about sixty years old, striking in appearance, with curly silver-gray hair framing her face.

"I'm Mrs. Merrill," she introduced herself, smiling warmly. "I presume you're the students from Starhurst who are going to put on a musical."

"Yes, we are," said Louise, recovering from her surprise. She introduced each of the girls.

"I'm very happy to meet all of you," Mrs. Merrill said. "I came to tell you I may have made a dreadful mistake. When I told Mrs. Crandall I would be glad to lend you the theater, I completely forgot I was waiting to hear from a traveling opera company about renting it."

The girls' faces showed their disappointment. Noticing this, Mrs. Merrill added contritely, "Oh, dear, I really am sorry."

Jean explained how inadequate the school auditorium was for the crowd they expected. "Mozart Hall was the perfect answer to our problem," she concluded.

"I'll tell you how we'll settle the problem," said Mrs. Merrill. "I'll give the traveling opera company one more week to decide. Then, if I don't hear from them, I'll consider the matter closed and you girls can have Mozart Hall."

"Thank you very much," Louise said fervently, and the others echoed her sentiments.

As Mrs. Merrill was about to leave, Doris said in a trembling voice, "We saw a-a ghost up in the third gallery. Do you——"

Before the girl could finish the sentence, the owner of the opera house laughed lightly and patted Doris on the shoulder. "An old theater, especially an unused one, is reputed to have ghosts of its deceased former actors, coming back to visit. There is nothing to worry about."

Jean asked her to explain why the dummies were standing about. Mrs. Merrill said she had had them placed there to provide atmosphere.

The woman said good-by, threw a kiss, and disappeared through the same wing she had entered. Soon the girls heard a door close.

Jean remarked, "She's a delightfully unexplainable person. Of course there's no truth in what she says about ghosts around this place being those of former actors."

The girls, though discouraged at the possibility of not being able to use Mozart Hall, continued their tour of the opera house. Louise discovered a stairway leading underneath the stage to the basement and they all trooped down.

The place was dirty and full of cobwebs, but intriguing nevertheless. There were dressing rooms with numbers on the doors.

Underneath the auditorium was the vast properties room. The girls entered the musty interior. Their flashlights revealed rows of glass wardrobes in which hung costumes of all types.

"Oh, maybe we can find extra costumes here for our musical," Louise said.

She and the others examined the compartments and came across a whole showcase marked LOUIS XIV.

"What a find!" Jean exclaimed, gazing in admiration at the elaborate garments.

At that moment Evelyn began to sneeze. She continued until tears ran down her cheeks. "Let's get out of this dirty place," she begged.

The girls followed her past the costume section and into a larger area, where figures of various sizes, dressed in suits of armor, stood about. Some held spears in their gauntlets, and all had metal visors over their faces.

"Let's hurry!" Doris urged nervously. "This place gives me the creeps."

The words were hardly spoken when her flashlight shone on a knight at the far side of the room. "L-look!" she quavered.

The suit of armor was moving slowly across the floor!

As the girls watched, electrified, the figure in armor walked along the far wall of the properties room. Suddenly it stopped and turned to face them. A door behind the knight opened, then closed quickly.

"Louise!" Jean cried. "Somebody was in that suit of armor and slipped out!"

The sisters dashed across the room, pushed the metal-clad, hinged figure aside, and rushed out a door. Beyond was a flight of stairs that turned at right angles. From somewhere above came the sound of running footsteps, then a door banged shut. The Danas leaped up the steps two at a time.

At the top of the stairway was an outside door.

Louise and Jean flung it open and peered into an alley that led to the street, but saw no one.

"Wait here, Jean!" said Louise. "I'll see if I can find the person who ran out."

She raced to the street but found nobody who looked the least suspicious. Louise asked an elderly woman if she had seen anyone running from the opera house.

"No, miss."

Disappointed, Louise returned to Jean. "Do you suppose it was the same person who played ghost in the gallery?"

Jean shrugged. "Louise, it looks as if we have a real mystery on our hands. If we don't solve it, we'll never get the cast to come here."

"You're right," her sister agreed.

The two joined the other girls, who were still in the properties room. Doris insisted that they go back to school at once. She was finally persuaded to stay, however, and the group continued to look around. After touring the rest of the basement, they climbed the stairs and went onstage again.

"This arrangement is really old-fashioned," Evelyn commented. "If we do put on our show here, we'll need flymen to hoist the scenery."

Ann giggled. "I guess we can find a few boys to help."

"Look at those huge sandbags!" Louise remarked, pointing to the sacks used as weights to counterbalance the scenery when it was high above the stage. "I'd hate to have one fall on me!"

Margaret Glenn was the first to notice two small open sections in the floor at the front of the stage. They looked like trap doors, their semi-hooded lids raised on the auditorium side of the square opening. She asked if anyone knew what these were used for.

"They're prompters' boxes," said Louise. "The prompter stands on a platform on the floor below so that only his head is above the stage. The raised lid of the box hides him from the audience.

Jean had walked over to one and beamed her light down inside. "This one has been closed."

Her classmates went to look at it. About six inches below the lid, boards had been installed so that the prompter's box now looked like a little chest.

Ann Freeman hurried across the stage to examine the other prompter's box. "This one hasn't been filled in," she declared.

Kneeling down, Ann looked inside the prompter's box. Suddenly she cried out in fright!

CHAPTER III

Ransacked Room

"What's the matter?" Louise asked, rushing to Ann's side.

"I-I just saw a horrible-looking person in the prompter's box!" Ann gasped. "He was staring right at me!"

Louise stooped and beamed her light into the opening. She saw no one. She listened intently for some sound from below, but heard nothing. "What did this person look like?" she asked Ann.

"Oh—hideous—like a gargoyle!"

"Well, no human being could be that ugly," declared Louise. "Whoever it was must have been wearing a mask from the properties room."

Jean chuckled. "If Lettie has been doing all these odd things," she said, "she's a lot more clever than I've given her credit for."

"Lettie or no Lettie, this settles it," Doris spoke

up. "You couldn't keep me in this place another moment, no matter how hard you try."

By this time the others also were a little shaken by the afternoon's sinister events and agreed to leave. They hurried through the auditorium and out the immense front door.

"There must be some sensible explanation for everything that happened," Louise said. "I suggest that we call on Mrs. Merrill and ask her point-blank."

"You go, and tell me about it later," said Doris. "I think there are too many of us to call on her at once, anyway. Jean, why don't you join Louise?"

The sisters nodded and promised to let the other girls know what they found out. Mrs. Merrill opened the door of her ornate, old-fashioned house.

She expressed surprise and delight at seeing Louise and Jean, then led them into the living room. The modern furnishings were a startling contrast to the outside of the house. The woman was having tea and insisted that the girls join her.

"Did you see any more ghosts?" she asked.

"We certainly did," Jean told her, then related the eerie events that had taken place after Mrs. Merrill had left Mozart Hall.

The woman frowned slightly, then looked off into space for several seconds. It almost seemed as if she were in a trance. The Danas stared at each other, puzzled. Did Mrs. Merrill know something about the ghostly doings?

Finally the woman turned to the girls once more, but still did not speak. Louise said, "I've heard there's some mystery connected with Mozart Hall."

The former opera star shuddered, then replied, "I suppose you mean the disappearance of my jewelry some years ago."

"Please tell us about it," Jean urged.

Mrs. Merrill said the incident had occurred eight years before, when she was singing in her last role at a performance in the old opera house. The part called for her to appear bedecked with jewelry. To celebrate the special occasion, she had taken a fabulous set of heirloom jewels from her safe-deposit box and had worn them that evening.

"While I was standing in the wings," she went on, "all the lights suddenly went out. A moment later a shot was fired from the stage. There were screams and a great deal of confusion. I fainted."

"Was anyone injured?" Louise asked.

"No," the singer replied. "The only thing that really happened was that in the hubbub my valuable gems were removed."

"How dreadful!" Louise exclaimed.

"The jewels have never been found," Mrs. Merrill continued. "All the actors and actresses were exonerated by the police, and so were the people who worked backstage."

"Did the police turn up any clues as to who the thief was?" Louise questioned.

Mrs. Merrill said no. There had been a theory that someone in the audience had managed to get backstage to commit the crime.

"That is a mystery," Louise commented. "I'm sorry you've never recovered your precious heirlooms, Mrs. Merrill."

The woman admitted that although eight years had gone by she still felt heartsick about the stolen gems.

"The pieces of jewelry," she said, "included several necklaces of pearls, diamonds, and rubies, three rings, and two bracelets. They were irreplaceable. The jewelry had once belonged to a French queen and had been given to the Merrill family for an outstanding act of chivalry by one of the male members. The gems were specially designed in an intricate pattern and set with flawless stones."

As Mrs. Merrill finished telling the story, a tall, slender man, about sixty years old and wearing an unhappy expression, walked into the room. He ran his hand through his thin gray hair as he said, "Mrs. Merrill, I got to go now."

"All right, Toby," she said.

Mrs. Merrill introduced him to the Danas as

Toby Grimes, her handyman and watchman for the opera house. He and the maid constituted her household. The girls acknowledged the introduction. Then, sensing that perhaps he and his employer would like to have a private conversation, the sisters said they must leave.

Toby Grimes followed them to the front door. He opened it and said in an unpleasant whisper, "If you girls expect me to clean that opera house before you use it, you have another guess coming. Do it yourselves or use it dirty!"

Louise and Jean were too amazed at his uncouth remark to reply. They walked back to their dormitory.

"Well, this has been quite an afternoon," Louise said, as they mounted the stairs to their rooms.

"Yes, it will be a relief to relax," Jean said. When she opened the door, she cried out, "Oh, what has happened here?"

Louise rushed in after her sister. Their study was a shambles. Bureau and desk drawers had been pulled out and the contents were strewn on the floor.

Jean's outburst brought Evelyn Starr on the run. She looked in dismay at the wreckage, then asked what it was all about.

"I don't know," Louise replied. "But it's obvious that whoever did it was after something of ours."

At once the Danas began to check for jewelry, keepsakes, and cash that had been in the drawers. None of these was missing.

"If this was supposed to be a prank," Jean said, frowning, "it was a nasty one."

At that moment Louise discovered that the sheets of music on which she and Jean had been working were gone from the bureau drawer where the girls had hidden them.

"Well, I think this has gone far enough," Evelyn said angrily. "I'm going to tell Mrs. Crandall about it."

Louise and Jean begged her not to, insisting they wanted to solve the mystery themselves. Despite the Danas' protests, Evelyn marched down to the headmistress's office and reported what had happened.

That evening Mrs. Crandall had all the students assemble in the lounge. After relating what had taken place, she stopped speaking for a moment and looked sternly around the room.

"This is a disgraceful affair," she resumed. "I would appreciate any information you girls can give about the person or persons who entered and ransacked the Danas' suite."

At once there was a buzz of conversation among the students, but no one offered any information. When they were dismissed, the girls gathered in small groups to discuss the incident. Louise and

Jean were sure that Lettie, for some motive of her own, was in back of the whole affair.

Just before the study bell rang, the Danas were surprised to see Lettie and her friend Ina Mason enter Mrs. Crandall's office. As the sisters passed the half-closed door, they were shocked to hear their names.

Lettie was saying in a loud voice, "I can give you a good clue as to who messed up Jean and Louise's room. Ina and I saw a man climbing up a ladder to the Danas' windows."

"Why didn't you report this?" Mrs. Crandall asked, startled.

"At the time we thought he was a window washer," Lettie replied.

"There was no work being done on the outside of the building today," the headmistress stated.

"Then the man must have been a burglar," Lettie said. She began to giggle. "Mrs. Crandall, I don't think he was after the song Louise and Jean were writing."

"But the Danas told me that it is the only thing missing," Mrs. Crandall said.

Lettie assumed an air of great importance that made the Danas wince. "Mrs. Crandall, you know Louise and Jean call themselves detectives. They study books on the subject and have all kinds of tools and gadgets that detectives use—and also burglars. It's my personal opinion that the thief was looking for tools," Lettie concluded smugly.

Outside in the hall, Louise and Jean could stand Lettie's lies no longer. Indignantly they rushed into Mrs. Crandall's office.

"I'm sorry to intrude," said Jean, fire in her eyes. "We couldn't help but overhear Lettie's unjust remarks. Mrs. Crandall, what she said about us is not true!"

The headmistress raised her eyebrows. "Do you mean none of it is true?" she asked.

Louise spoke up. "We don't know about the man on the ladder," she admitted. "But the part about the books and our having burglars' tools around is completely false."

"What have you to say to this, Lettie?" Mrs. Crandall asked.

Lettie began to squirm. She looked at Ina, then out the window.

Finally Ina stammered, "M-maybe Lettie was exaggerating a little. But really, Mrs. Crandall, we did see a man climbing a ladder toward the Danas' rooms."

Mrs. Crandall said that the watchman had been home ill that day. Unfortunately she had not been able to secure the services of another person. "So it is possible that an intruder ransacked the Danas' suite," she concluded.

When the conference ended, the Danas were more determined than ever to solve the mystery. Why should anyone want to take their song?

Evelyn Starr was inclined to think it was another one of Lettie and Ina's wild stories.

"Well, it doesn't really matter," said Louise. "Jean and I will just have to sit down and make another copy of 'We're All Mysterious.'"

The girls made no secret of the fact that they were writing their song again and would deliver it to Miss Rosemont. After dinner the next evening they went across the campus to the faculty house where Miss Rosemont lived.

"My, how dark it's grown all of a sudden," Louise remarked as they walked along. "I guess it's going to rain."

"Yes. We'd better hurry."

The sisters took a short cut, which brought them to the rear of the faculty house. The back porch light was on.

"Louise," Jean whispered suddenly, "I thought I saw someone move behind those bushes over there."

Before her sister had a chance to reply, a man wearing a long robe and a stocking over his head and face dashed from the shrubbery directly toward the girls.

"Stop!" he ordered in a low voice.

CHAPTER IV

A Mystery Song

As Louise and Jean stood, mystified by the command from the disguised man, four smaller figures, definitely girls, darted from the shadows. They were similarly dressed. The Danas were surrounded!

There was a suppressed giggle from one of the smaller figures. Louise and Jean guessed at once that they must be students.

"Now!" one of the smaller figures commanded.

The next instant, Louise and Jean were swept off their feet and carried away. In the rush, someone grabbed the music from Louise's hand. She demanded that it be given back, but her tormentors paid no attention.

Out of the corner of one eye she saw the disguised man disappear among the trees. He was carrying some papers in his hand.

Louise and Jean were struggling to free them-

selves, but resistance was useless. They were out-
numbered and their captors were strong and wiry.

"Where are you taking us?" Jean demanded.

The only answer was a ripple of laughter from
the group. In a few moments the Danas knew
what was in store for them. A ducking in the
campus pond!

"Ready! One! Two! Three!" one of the disguised figures cried out.

Louise and Jean were swung back and forth
several times, like a hammock, then tossed into
the water. It was chilly and the sisters shivered as
they went under. By the time they rose to the
surface, the pranksters had vanished.

"We sure let ourselves in for that," Jean said
unhappily, as she and Louise swam to the edge of
the pool and climbed out.

Bedraggled and chilled, they decided to return
to the dormitory. Jean was angry, but Louise was
more perplexed than disturbed.

"Who could that man have been?" she asked.
"I think he was the one who took the music."

"Maybe the ladder climber, Louise. And who
were the girls? If they're Starhurst students, we
may never find out."

"They did have a good head start getting away,"
Louise conceded. "But don't be discouraged, Jean.
Perhaps they left a clue someplace."

As the Danas hurried along, they continued to
discuss the unexplainable affair. They came to the

conclusion that it was more than a prank; other-
wise, the man would not have been involved.

For some reason unknown to the sisters, a person, or persons, was trying to keep them from
turning in their song for the contest. Was there
more to it than just jealousy on the part of another
contestant, perhaps Lettie?

"Do you think we should tell Mrs. Crandall?"
Jean suggested.

Louise thought this over, then said, "Not yet,
just in case the whole thing was Lettie's idea."

After Louise and Jean had showered and put on
pajamas and robes, they studied for two hours.
When the bell rang for the half-hour relaxation
period before bedtime, they called Evelyn and
Doris into their study. Louise told them what had
happened.

The four girls held a council of war, determined
to find out who had so unceremoniously given the
Danas the ducking. With the assistance of three
other friends, the group toured the dormitory,
asking and searching for clues. But when the re-
tirement bell rang, they had learned nothing. The
next morning brought no further solution.

"I'll never be satisfied until I find out who was
responsible for last night's incident," said Jean.

"I won't either," Louise agreed. "This afternoon we have our piano lessons at Miss Rosemont's house. Let's ask her if we may stay there
afterward and write our song. We'll turn it in

then and there, before anybody can get it."

"Fine idea," said Jean, her good humor restored.

Miss Rosemont agreed to the plan. After their piano session, she suggested that the Danas go upstairs to her bedroom and work while she instructed other students.

The sisters divided the work. As Louise wrote out the title, "We're All Mysterious," she remarked that this was becoming more appropriate every minute.

It was five o'clock when she and Jean went downstairs with the finished copy. As they turned the song over to Miss Rosemont, she said, "How about playing and singing it for me now?"

Louise sat down at the piano and after a short introduction, Jean started to sing.

> I can't figure you out,
> You can't figure me out,
> Both of us so blue—
> Till you drop a clue,
> I drop a clue,
> That we would be true.
>
> We have little quarrels,
> Such important quarrels,
> Can't figure them out—
> First you forgive,
> Then I forgive,
> Wonder what it's all about.

You're so mysterious,
I'm so mysterious,
We need a clue or two—
I give a hint,
You give a hint,
No one else will ever do.

We smile and both agree
We've solved a mystery
Old as the stars above—
We're all delirious,
Yet so mysterious,
When we're in love.

At the conclusion Miss Rosemont clapped enthusiastically. "That's very good," she praised the girls. "I'd say good enough to publish."

Louise and Jean, blushing in their excitement, smiled. Miss Rosemont continued, "But I think it is only fair to tell you that several other excellent songs have been turned in, and I expect more. Competition is a fine thing."

The sisters nodded and Louise remarked, "I guess everybody likes to win a contest, but just writing the song was fun, too."

The music teacher said that she was amazed at the talent being shown by the Starhurst students. "It will be difficult for the judges to choose the four songs to be sung in the musical."

"When will winners be announced?" Jean asked.

"About the middle of May. There will be a great deal of rehearsing, and if we're to have dancing or some other features to go with the original songs, these will take time to work out."

In a few minutes, the girls left and returned to the dormitory. They went to pick up their mail.

On a bulletin board beside the boxes was a notice of an assembly the following afternoon for the whole student body. Miss Parker, one of the history teachers, would give a talk on the history of the theater.

"That should be very interesting," Louise remarked to her sister.

"Interesting nothing!" said an unpleasant voice behind them. They recognized it at once as that of Lettie Briggs. "I'm not going to go."

"I'd say that this is required," Jean said.

Lettie tossed her head defiantly, then gave a smug smile. "I'll twist my ankle or something," she said as she unlocked her mailbox. "Oh, two letters! One from Joe and one from John."

Jean impishly leaned over to see the handwriting, but Lettie hugged the letters to her chest and rushed off. The Danas giggled but said nothing. They knew that Lettie was always bragging about dates that never materialized.

It was with some amusement that Louise and Jean, seated with several of their friends the next afternoon, watched Lettie and Ina come into the school auditorium.

"Lettie isn't even hobbling!" Jean exclaimed. "I guess that ankle business didn't work."

Soon Miss Parker walked onto the platform. The slender young woman smiled warmly and began her talk.

"The history of the drama and theater is probably as old as man himself," she said. "I presume that at some time in his life, everyone has a desire to be a performer.

"In ancient days the so-called plays were always religious and many people took part. First a few men of a tribe would sing and dance in honor of their gods. Later, the whole audience would participate."

The teacher went on to say that these religious plays became more and more elaborate, particularly in the days of ancient Greece and Rome, and during the Middle Ages. They were always held outdoors. The theater building came into vogue only a few centuries ago.

"The problems in these old theaters were many," Miss Parker continued. "One of them concerned the lighting. In the beginning torches were used. Then oil and gas lamps became popular. But these were not satisfactory. Oil lamps were smelly, and in the gas lamps the pressure often failed, extinguishing the lights. In cold climates there was a heating problem. Stoves were inadequate.

"Audiences changed with the times, too. Formerly there was a great deal of heckling of actors. When anyone didn't like a performance, he did not hesitate to throw eggs or tomatoes onto the stage. Many a curtain was rung down to avoid a riot.

"Some of the opera houses became very elaborate in their furnishings, as a few of you girls have found out from Mozart Hall. And the men and women who attended the performances dressed very elegantly in velvet, satins, and furs.

"But behind the scenes the story was quite different. Men worked hard in their shirt sleeves, raising the heavy pieces of scenery and lowering them. Electricians often coped frantically with bulky, old-fashioned lighting systems.

"One of the most interesting jobs was that of the sound-effects men. They invented all sorts of clever ways to imitate the sounds of rain and snow, rushing water, and thunder. Today it is usually done by playing records.

"It was in the theater that the expression 'Stealing my thunder' was born. In 1708 a man named John Dennis, a theater critic, devised a new method of making thunder. Before that it had been accomplished by rolling lead balls on the floor or in a wooden trough.

"Dennis's invention was a sheet of copper hung vertically on a stick with a handle at the bottom. This was shaken violently and gave a very realistic effect. Many people began to copy Dennis's invention, and he, complaining bitterly, used to remark that people were 'stealing his thunder.' "

The Starhurst students laughed. Then Miss Parker went on to tell how other effects had been accomplished in the theater in the old days. Sea spray, for example, had been created by flinging up handfuls of rice from the floor between two sections of ocean scenery.

After presenting many more interesting facts, Miss Parker concluded her talk by mentioning sections of the old-time stage, like those the Danas had already seen at Mozart Hall. One place the girls had not noticed, however, was the secret opening at the back of the stage through which the manager could watch the audience and the musicians.

When the lecture was over, Louise looked thoughtfully at Jean. "Do you suppose," she said, "that there is such a place backstage at Mozart Hall? If there is, it might explain a lot about where the ghost may hide at times."

"You're right!" Jean said. "Let's go down there and find out!"

CHAPTER V

Crash in the Dark

"THE first chance we have let's visit Mozart Hall and see if there's a secret opening at the back of the stage," Louise said to Jean as they left the school auditorium.

The girls went to their suite. The door to the study was open. When they walked in, the sisters were surprised to find Fritzi. She was intently gazing at a drawing on Louise's desk.

"Why, Fritzi!" Louise exclaimed.

The maid looked up, startled. "I-I beg your pardon. I wanted to—ask you—"

The Danas waited for her to go on, but as she stood there, confused and unable to speak, Louise prompted her. "You wanted to ask us——?"

"Yes," Fritzi said finally. "I left a dustcloth up here. While I was looking for it, I saw the sketch on the desk. Is this the way you find lost things— make a drawing?"

Louise smiled. She told the maid that the drawing was one she had done of the interior of Mozart Hall.

"We have to clean the theater before we can use it. I thought this sketch would make it easier to plan our work."

"I see," said Fritzi. "This is Mozart Hall, did you say? Oh, I think it's wonderful. Would you please give it to me?"

"Why, I guess so," Louise said. "I can easily make another."

"Oh, thank you," Fritzi cried, delighted. She picked up the sketch and left the room.

"I wish you hadn't done that," Jean said.

"Why?"

Jean explained that Fritzi, who appeared to be a dense person, was really rather mysterious. With the strange happenings at Mozart Hall, it might have been unwise to give the maid a map of the place.

Louise felt no such qualms. "I'm sure no harm will come of it."

Jean, however, could not put Fritzi out of her mind and after dinner went to see Mrs. Crandall. Cleverly the girl brought up the subject of the maid without revealing her suspicions.

"She's slow, but perfectly honest," the headmistress said. "She has very good references."

As the days went by, school studies, activities, and rehearsals for the musical prevented the Danas from going to the opera house for nearly a week. When they did go, Evelyn Starr and Ann Freeman went along.

As the great front door to Mozart Hall squeaked open, the girls' hearts began to beat faster. Would they see the ghost again?

"Where shall we go first?" Evelyn asked.

"Let's investigate backstage," Louise suggested. "Maybe we can locate the manager's secret opening."

The girls started down one of the side aisles in single file. Jean was in the lead, playing her flashlight ahead. Halfway to the stage, she looked up to the third gallery.

"Nothing there," she told herself. "But maybe —oh!"

Jean had stepped into a hole, twisting her ankle. She lost her balance and fell to the floor. Ann, who was a few feet behind her, rushed to Jean's assistance.

"What happened?" Ann asked, as the others came up.

With a wry face, Jean sat up and turned her flashlight into the hole, which Ann had barely missed stepping into herself. The depression was nearly three feet square and six inches deep at the sides. It tapered down to a screen over the opening of a duct. Jean's foot had struck high on the side, wrenching her ankle.

"I guess there used to be a heat register here,"

Jean said. "But why would anyone take the grating off?" she mused, rubbing her ankle.

"Let's talk about you, sis, instead of the register," Louise spoke up. "How does your ankle feel?"

"Tell you in a minute," Jean replied, pulling herself up. She took a few steps and said, "It doesn't feel too bad."

At that moment, Evelyn discovered the grating of the register. It was leaning against a seat nearby. She and Louise put it in place.

The group speculated on why the grating had been removed. If something were wrong with the heating system, why was it being repaired now? The opera house was going to be used only for the month of June—at least that was the length of time the traveling company had wanted to rent it.

Jean assured the girls that she felt able to proceed with the tour. She suggested they forget the stage for a while and go to the basement.

"I'd like to find out what possible connection the heating system may have with the mystery of this place."

The girls went to a side corridor and descended a stairway. They had gone down only a few steps when Louise exclaimed, "Look!"

She pointed to a section of the wooden wall that had been hacked out. Apparently it had once been a door that had been paneled over.

"Somebody must have been looking here for a

hidden object," Evelyn remarked. "Probably under the register, too. I wonder if it could have been Toby Grimes and if he had any luck."

The Danas were puzzled. They were suddenly reminded of Fritzi and her marked interest in the Mozart Hall drawing. But immediately they concluded that the maid was hardly shrewd enough to tackle such a search herself.

The girls went on down the stairway. Confronting them in the stone foundation below was another large hole. The masonry had been removed from an area about three feet in diameter.

"Now I'm sure someone has been searching for something," Jean said. "But what could it be?"

"Probably nothing more important than an electrician testing the wiring system of the building," Evelyn said, chuckling.

"Maybe you're right," Jean conceded as the girls walked on, looking for the furnace room.

They found it, but were disappointed. The place revealed no clues to the mystery of the register.

"Let's go back and investigate the stage," Louise proposed. Before anyone could move, she said, "Listen!"

The girls stood stock-still. Suddenly they could hear a voice singing a soft, plaintive melody somewhere in Mozart Hall!

Louise whispered, "It's a coloratura soprano! Can the opera-house ghost be a woman?"

The group decided that the strange singing was undoubtedly coming from the stage. It was being carried down to them through the flue between the auditorium and the furnace.

"Do you suppose Mrs. Merrill could be singing?" Jean suggested.

"Let's tiptoe up and find out," Evelyn urged. "Maybe now we'll solve the mystery of the ghost!"

As silently as possible, the girls retraced their steps to the main floor. Without making a sound, they crossed the corridor and entered the auditorium. The singing continued. Now there was no question but that it came from the dark stage.

The girls, not daring to flick on their lights, advanced cautiously, listening to the unfamiliar melody. It had a haunting, almost fearful quality.

Suddenly there was a tremendous crash on the stage. The singing stopped abruptly, then a high-pitched scream rang out.

"What—and who—was that?" Evelyn gasped.

"Come on!" Jean cried. "Let's find out!"

She flashed on her light and ran down the aisle toward the stage. The other girls followed, each with her own flashlight turned on. Jean mounted the platform and beamed her light around the pieces of scenery. Nobody. She and Evelyn dashed into the wing on the right side of the stage, while Louise and Ann ran to the left. No one was hiding in either section.

The singing stopped. There was a crash and a scream.

"What fell?" Evelyn asked. "It sounded like an atom bomb!"

Jean shrugged.

As the girls met again in the center of the stage, Louise said, "Perhaps we shouldn't stay here. There are too many heavy pieces around that could be dropped on us. We'd better go."

"That's, no doubt, exactly what someone wants us to do," Jean remarked. "You know, I think this ghost business is being put on just to keep us out of Mozart Hall!"

"But why?" Evelyn queried.

"I feel someone's searching for a precious article and doesn't want us around," Jean said.

Louise agreed and added that it might even be dangerous to hold the musical in Mozart Hall.

"All the more reason for us to solve the mystery before then," Jean reminded her.

She suggested they go to Mrs. Merrill's home and talk to her once more about the ghost incidents. They left the opera house and went next door.

"How delightful of you to call!" Mrs. Merrill exclaimed. "No doubt you've come to ask me if I've heard from the opera company. I haven't, and they have only a few days more. I'm inclined to think that no word will come from them. So you girls may as well go ahead and make plans for putting on your show."

"That's very kind," said Louise, and the others

also expressed their appreciation. After a moment's hesitation, Louise went on, "What we came to talk to you about, Mrs. Merrill, is another matter in connection with the opera house. Each time we've been there, something spooky has happened."

Mrs. Merrill began to chuckle. "Are you going to tell me you saw a ghost again?"

Louise shook her head but mentioned the recent mysterious incidents.

Mrs. Merrill frowned. "A crash? Well, that I can understand. The building is old and chunks of loose plaster may have fallen. But the singing and a scream!"

The one-time opera star paused dramatically, then continued dreamily, "The very walls of that theater have music in them. I honestly believe, though, that the wind whistling through a crack was the cause of the plaintive sounds you heard."

It became evident to the girls that Mrs. Merrill was not going to admit anything unusual had occurred in her beloved Mozart Hall. Changing the subject, she asked how rehearsals for the musical were coming along. The girls answered her questions and then rose to leave.

As they were saying good-by at the front door, Jean caught a glimpse of Toby Grimes turning into the alley between the opera house and Mrs. Merrill's home. Eager to question him, she hurried after the man.

"Oh, Mr. Grimes!" Jean called. "Have you been in the theater this afternoon?"

"No, I haven't. Why?"

Jean then told him what had happened and wondered if he could explain it.

"I certainly can't," Toby snapped. "And what's more, if you think it's so dangerous in there, why don't you stay out?" With a show of anger he added loudly, "I do my job as caretaker and I don't want you saying anything to the contrary."

"I didn't say that you weren't doing your job," Jean replied calmly. "I just thought maybe you could explain why Mozart Hall is so spooky."

The caretaker declared that the opera house was not spooky and that he took good care of the place. "I can't be wasting any more time with your foolish questions," he concluded brusquely.

With that, he turned and hurried down the alley. Jean went back to the others and remarked that the caretaker was just as mysterious in his way as Mrs. Merrill was in hers.

"They're baffling, all right," Evelyn said. "Almost as baffling as the old opera house itself."

As the four friends turned their steps toward Starhurst, they talked of the monthly dance, which was scheduled for the following evening.

"I almost forgot about it," Louise said.

"Ken Scott wouldn't be flattered to hear that," Evelyn teased. "Wait till we tell him that singing ghosts are his latest competition!"

Louise grinned and said that she would give him her full attention to make up for it.

Louise and Jean dated two good-looking roommates from Walton Academy, nearby. Ken was a little more reserved than Chris Barton, who was Jean's date.

"By the way, the boys are coming early," Louise said. "Why don't we show them around Mozart Hall? They'd love to see the ghost in the gallery!"

"They sure would," Jean agreed. "Let's do it!"

The following afternoon, when the girls returned to their suite to prepare for the dance, they found a telephone message on Jean's desk. It read:

Ken Scott and Chris Barton called to say they are sorry to miss the dance tonight. They hope to be invited next month.

CHAPTER VI

An Accusation

STUNNED by the message from the boys, Louise and Jean flopped on the couch in their study.

"This means we can't go to the dance!" Jean wailed.

Louise thought, What could have happened to make Ken and Chris change their minds?

"Ken just wouldn't do a rude thing like this," said Louise. "Waiting till the last minute to say he can't come!"

"No, it isn't like Chris, either," Jean said, then added hopefully, "Maybe this note is a hoax. I'll call Chris and find out."

"Oh, Jean, don't do that," Louise begged.

"Why not?"

Louise, by nature very understanding, said she preferred not to call. "The boys may have a perfectly good reason for breaking the date," she pointed out. "If so, asking them directly might be embarrassing."

Jean did not agree. She phoned Walton Academy and learned that both boys were away for the weekend. There was a sudden tightness in her throat and she bit her lip to keep from crying.

Louise had overheard the conversation and tried to ease the pain for her sister. Jean was not to be soothed. "If those boys think they're coming to our dance next month," she said, "they're in for a shock. I'll never invite them!"

At that moment Doris Harland came into the room. "My goodness!" she exclaimed. "What's the matter? You two look as though you've lost your last friend."

"Not quite that," Louise replied. "But right at this moment it's almost as bad. No dates for tonight." She told Doris what had happened.

"Why, the old meanies!" Doris said. "Well, don't worry. I'll soon fix everything."

Without explaining she left the room. Ten minutes later Doris burst into the Danas' study and told the sisters that she had arranged for two blind dates. "You'll like the boys," she said. "They're good dancers."

It was true that the Danas' dates turned out to be excellent dancers. But this was all that saved the evening from being a total disappointment to the sisters. Jean's partner talked of nothing but the many athletic honors he had won. Louise's escort was constantly making puns at which he laughed before anyone else did.

"And they aren't even funny," Louise confided to Evelyn during refreshments.

The Danas were glad when the evening was over and they tumbled into bed.

Sunday morning a notice appeared on the bulletin board stating that after Vespers that evening the four winners in the song contest would be announced. There was great speculation and excitement among the students.

Lettie Briggs bragged loudest. "I know I'm going to win," she declared.

"What makes you so sure?" Evelyn asked.

"You just wait until you hear my song," Lettie said. "It's a natural—a hit tune."

The Danas and their friends looked at one another in disgust. They were glad when the time came to attend church services in Penfield. At least for a while they would not have to listen to Lettie's boasting! But on the way back to Starhurst the subject came up again.

"Lettie and her claims to fame remind me," Louise said, "that we've never solved the mystery of the dunking incident, which we think she engineered."

"That's right," Jean agreed. "I'm still mad about that."

"And I'd also like to know who that man was who took our music," Louise added.

She suggested that perhaps the captors' outfits were choir robes borrowed from Starhurst.

"You're probably right, sis."

"Let's ask Miss Rosemont if we can look at the school's robes," Jean suggested.

After midday dinner, the Danas contacted the music director and were granted permission to inspect the choir robes. They were kept in the third-floor storeroom at the music hall.

The girls hurried to the building and located the room, which opened off a small corridor near a back stairway.

"I never knew this place existed," Jean remarked.

"Nor I," Louise said. "Why, anyone could have come up here and sneaked the choir robes down this stairway without being seen!"

Jean tried the door. Fortunately, it was unlocked. Entering, she snapped on the light. Louise followed her inside and went to the rack where the robes were hanging.

The Danas examined each one and found none with wrinkles.

"These certainly weren't used by our captors," Louise observed.

"You're right. Another false clue!" Jean groaned in disappointment.

Louise thought for a while, then said, "You know, it's possible these could have been used recently and were brushed and pressed before being put back."

Jean nodded. "But I guess that rules out Lettie. She wouldn't be caught using a clothesbrush and iron. Lettie and hard work just don't mix!"

Louise smiled. "I agree wholeheartedly. But Lettie might have asked someone else to do the job—even paid her for doing it."

"Meaning?"

"Fritzi Brunner, perhaps."

As the sisters discussed this new angle, they concluded that there was no point in asking the maid directly. Even if Louise's hunch was right, Fritzi would deny it. The Danas must learn the truth some other way.

"Do you suppose," Jean mused, "that the disguised man could be a friend of Fritzi's?"

"Possibly," Louise conceded. She walked around the clothes rack and suddenly exclaimed, "Jean, look here! A clue, maybe!"

On the floor lay a small, ragged clipping that had been torn from a newspaper. It was a dress-sale ad. *The paper was dated two days before the disguised figures had tossed Louise and Jean into the pond!*

"It certainly looks as if these were the choir robes they used!" Jean cried excitedly. "With this evidence, I think we should question Fritzi."

The sisters discussed the matter further as they walked back to their dormitory. They decided not to speak to Fritzi yet. She might repeat a mixed-up version of the story.

After Vespers the girls gathered in the lounge. An excited buzz of anticipation rose. Soon they would hear the results of the contest.

Once more Lettie began to brag that she knew her song would be one of those chosen. Ina Mason and a few of Lettie's friends agreed, but the rest of the student body ignored the girl's conceited remarks.

Presently Miss Rosemont walked to the front of the room. As she began to speak, a hush descended. Many hearts began to beat a little faster. No one wanted to miss a single word.

After giving the names of the judges, including that of Mrs. Crandall, the music director said, "We have all been amazed at the musical talent revealed at Starhurst. Unfortunately only four songs can be selected to be used in *Spring Is Here*.

"In reaching a decision, the committee has taken several factors into account. The main one is how appropriately the words fit into the theme of the musical. Another factor is the originality of the melody. With so many songs to choose from, we picked those that in no way even hinted of familiar tunes, old or new.

"It gives me great pleasure, therefore——" Miss Rosemont paused and the girls leaned forward expectantly. The teacher resumed, "—to announce that one of the songs we decided upon was written by Marian Smith. Marian, will you please play and sing your piece?"

The applause was loud. Marian, flushed and excited, made her way to the piano. At the conclusion of her lilting number, the response was even more enthusiastic.

"The second winner," said Miss Rosemont, as the room became quiet again, "is Dorothy Tompkins, who has written a duet. She will play, and two of her friends from the glee club, Sonja and Hildegarde, will sing."

When the three performers finished, Louise, clapping loudly, turned to Jean and whispered, "Dotty's duet is excellent. If other songs are this good, I'm afraid we don't stand a chance."

When the applause died down, the music director announced that another winner was Helen Brownley. The girl's song turned out to be a humorous one, which produced much giggling among the students. The number would surely make a hit in the musical.

Now there was only one more winner to be announced! As Miss Rosemont again faced the students, the Dana girls held their breath!

"Before I present the last winning song in our contest," she said, "I want to beg those of you who didn't win not to feel too disappointed. Your songs will be played and sung another time. Starhurst should be proud to have such an abundant crop of hit tunes!"

The girls smiled politely but wished the music director would hurry and announce the last winner. Sensing this, Miss Rosemont said, "The fourth and final winning song is a combination number. It has been written by Louise and Jean Dana and is entitled 'We're All Mysterious.' "

"Oh, that's wonderful!" cried Evelyn, hugging the delighted sisters, whose faces broke into pleased smiles.

"What an appropriate title to be written by our detectives!" said Dorothy Tompkins, who led the burst of applause for the Danas.

At Miss Rosemont's request, Louise played the music while Jean sang. At the end of their performance the applause was thunderous and several girls demanded an encore. Happily, the sisters went through the number once more. Again the clapping was tremendous.

Suddenly Lettie Briggs was on her feet. She was waving her arms wildly, trying to get Miss Rosemont's attention. But, in the cheers of enthusiasm for the Danas, no one listened to her.

"Let's have another chorus," somebody requested. "We'll all sing it." Louise and Jean, though a little breathless, gaily obliged.

By this time, Lettie was almost screaming at the top of her lungs. Finally the applause stopped and everyone turned to stare at her. They expected the unpleasant girl to complain that the contest was unfair because her entry had not been chosen. To their amazement, she had something totally different to say.

"Miss Rosemont," Lettie shrilled, "the Danas' song can't be used. It's not original! It's a steal!"

The student body was stunned. Louise and Jean, thunderstruck, were speechless for several seconds.

Then Jean cried out angrily, "That's not true, Lettie. Louise and I composed it—every single word and note!"

"That's what you claim," Lettie said haughtily, "but I heard the very same song over the local radio station a couple of mornings ago!"

CHAPTER VII

Strange Chiseling

"You heard what?" Louise exclaimed, shocked at Lettie's accusation. "You say it was Jean's and my song you picked up on the radio?"

Miss Rosemont informed Lettie that her charge was a very serious one. She would have to back up her statement with proof.

Lettie was in her element now. Not only did she love to have a large audience when she was speaking, but she was particularly pleased if her subject was damaging to someone else.

"I have a witness," Lettie said dramatically. "Ina, you heard it, too. Tell everybody that."

Ina did not seem to share her roommate's desire to be in the limelight. Looking extremely embarrassed, she apparently had no choice but to confirm Lettie's statement.

She said that two days before, she and Lettie had turned on their room radio. The song they had heard had a different name and the words were not exactly the same. But the tune was identical to the one Louise had just played.

Turning to the Danas, Miss Rosemont asked, "Are you sure you never heard this record?"

"Certainly!" the sisters replied together.

Mrs. Crandall, who had not been present at the session because of other school matters, was summoned. She was astounded to learn what Lettie and Ina had reported.

After a few moments' thought she said, "Under the circumstances, the committee will have to hold up its decision on the Danas' song until we have made a complete investigation." The headmistress looked at Louise and Jean. "I'm very sorry, girls," she added kindly.

A sober group left the lounge and went slowly to their rooms. Several friends of the Danas gathered in their study to talk over the humiliating affair.

They were equally divided in their theory about Lettie's accusation. Some felt that the mean girl had made up the story about having heard the Danas' song out of spite. But Jean, Louise, Evelyn, and Doris were inclined to think Lettie was telling the truth.

"I doubt that even Miss Troublemaker Briggs would be nervy enough to dream up a tale like that," Jean remarked.

"At any rate," Louise said, frowning, "we'll

have to do some quick sleuthing and get to the bottom of all this."

"Tell you what," Ann Freeman spoke up. "Let's take turns listening to the local radio station during most of the day. One of us is bound to hear the song Lettie's talking about."

"That's a good idea," Jean agreed.

Immediately the girls began to compare notes on classes, sports programs, and various extracurricular activities they had to attend. Finally it was worked out so that practically the entire following day could be covered.

After the Danas' friends had left, the sisters continued to talk about the amazing turn of events. Both were convinced it had something to do with the thefts of their sheet music.

"I'm going to track down the pirate who took it!" Jean said with determination.

"I'm with you," her sister said soberly. "We can't let him get away with this!"

Jean's usually sparkling eyes were troubled. "It might be days before any of us hear the record on the radio. And I hate to have so much time go by before we find the plagiarizer."

"How do you suppose news of our song leaked out in the first place?" Louise mused.

"I haven't the least idea, except that I'm beginning to think there really was a man who climbed a ladder to our room."

The next day radios were being played all over

the Starhurst campus. Though the students listened to record after record, "We're All Mysterious" was not among them.

In the late afternoon the Danas went for their mail. There were three letters in the box.

"One from Aunt Harriet," said Louise.

Jean took the other two pieces. One was addressed to her from Chris, the other to Louise from Ken.

The younger girl ripped open her envelope and exclaimed, "Louise, listen to this! Chris was informed that the dance was called off!"

Her sister's letter from Ken said practically the same thing. Someone had deliberately played a mean trick on the Danas!

"I'm going to call Chris at once," Jean said.

When the youth learned what had happened, he groaned. "You mean the dance wasn't postponed? And Ken and I missed a good party with you and Louise? Jean, I'll do everything I can to help you find out who was responsible. That sure was a low-down trick to play."

"How did you receive word that the dance had been postponed?" Jean asked.

Chris said that a telegram had come, addressed to him and Ken. It had been sent from Penfield and was signed *The Sisters*. "Anyway, it invited us to the next dance," Chris said hopefully.

Jean laughed. "Good. And after this, don't believe any more last-minute wires!"

The next day after classes Louise and Jean hurried down to the telegraph office in the center of town. The woman in charge, Mrs. Muller, listened to the girls' story.

"Why, how dreadful!" she exclaimed. "I'll look up the telegram at once."

When Mrs. Muller found the copy of the message, she said she had a hazy recollection of two girls having come in together. She had assumed they were sisters.

"I'll bet anything 'the sisters' were Lettie and Ina!" Jean said indignantly to Louise.

Mrs. Muller also recalled that the day before the telegram was sent the same two girls had torn several blank forms off a pad and put them in their handbags. They had not offered any explanation, nor had they sent a message.

The Danas thanked Mrs. Muller for her help and started for Starhurst. They saw Fritzie Brunner walking on the other side of the street. Jean and Louise crossed over.

"How's your detective work coming along?" Jean asked her, smiling.

Fritzi's eyes lighted up. "I'm trying awful hard," she replied. "I'm not having much luck, but I'm not giving up."

Louise said that there was a chance right now for the maid to do some real detective work.

"How's that?" Fritzi's voice squeaked with excitement.

"We're trying to trace a mysterious telegram," Jean explained. "We think one of the Starhurst girls sent it."

"Yes?"

"Fritzi"—Louise's tone became confidential—"did you come across some telegraph blanks at any time while you were cleaning the rooms?"

The maid did not reply. She seemed to be thinking hard.

"This is very important," Louise prompted her. "Were there some telegraph blanks—flat, crumpled, or torn—in any of the wastebaskets?"

Suddenly Fritzi giggled. "I guess I'm a detective at that," she said happily. "I remember now. There were a lot of half-scribbled, crunched-up telegrams in one of the rooms."

"Whose?" the Danas chorused.

"Lettie Briggs and Ina Mason's!"

The Danas could not hide their elation. They broke into laughter. "Fritzi, you are a detective! Thanks for the information," Jean said. "And I wish you luck with the rest of your sleuthing."

After the maid had walked on, the Danas saw Evelyn Starr coming along the street. They told her the story.

"Lettie ought to be punished!" Evelyn stormed. As she went off to do an errand, she could not get this thought out of her mind. Suddenly she found a phone booth and made a call. She talked for several minutes, then hung up.

Grinning, she headed for the telegraph office and wrote out a message. It said:

> Miss Lettie Briggs
> Miss Ina Mason
> Starhurst School
> Penfield
> We will come to call for you
> directly after dinner Thursday
> evening.
>
> The Brothers

Evelyn handed the message to Mrs. Muller, who read it, smiled, and said, "You're a friend of the Danas, aren't you? I hope your joke works."

The girl hoped so too and said to herself, "One of two things will happen: either Lettie will catch on that the Danas found out who sent the telegram signed 'The Sisters,' or she'll fall for the message in the telegram." Evelyn smiled. "I have a feeling she'll take the bait."

Meanwhile, Louise and Jean were approaching Mozart Hall. They were amazed to see Fritzi Brunner talking to Toby Grimes in front of the theater. They wondered whether she knew him, or had come on an errand for Mrs. Crandall.

Suddenly the handyman and the maid turned down the alleyway between the buildings. The girls concluded that Fritzi was going into the Merrill house by way of the back door.

"But maybe she isn't after all," said Louise suddenly. "Remember how interested Fritzi was in my sketch of the layout of Mozart Hall?"

"Let's find out," Jean urged.

The Danas rang the front doorbell of Mrs. Merrill's home. Her maid answered and told the girls that her mistress was not at home.

"Is Fritzi Brunner here?" Jean asked.

"No, ma'am," the maid replied. "I'm the only one here, and I don't know anyone by that name."

The sisters exchanged glances. Maybe Fritzi was in the opera house! Louise asked the maid if she would lend them a key to Mozart Hall and a flashlight.

"Certainly," said the girl, and went off to get the two articles. Returning, she handed them over. "This key is for the side door."

The Danas thanked her and hurried to the opera house. The side door opened into the auditorium. The instant the girls were inside and Louise had flicked on the flashlight, they could hear what sounded like someone chiseling stone.

"The stonework in the basement," Louise whispered. "Come on!"

The girls tiptoed up one side of the auditorium until they came to a door. They pulled it open and found a stairway leading downward. Below, there was a flickering light and the sound of the chiseling was louder.

"Shall we go on?" Jean suggested.

Louise was hesitant. As she stood still, trying to make a decision, a man's voice ordered, "Turn off that light!" The speaker was not Toby Grimes.

The sisters turned around. They saw no one. Instinctively Louise switched off her flash. The light at the foot of the stairs was also extinguished.

Jean whispered to Louise, "I guess he didn't mean us, but whoever is working below."

"Yes," Louise whispered back. "But it's probably so they won't be recognized. Which means they know we're in the building."

As the Danas remained in the doorway, listening intently, a slight noise suddenly directed their attention toward the stage. Jean stifled a cry and Louise clutched her sister's arm.

Moving across the platform was a white figure surrounded by a weird, phosphorescent light!

Louise and Jean, though unnerved and frightened, did not move. This was their chance to find out about the ghostly creature that flitted around Mozart Hall!

Now the eerie figure descended the steps from the stage and started up the aisle directly toward the Danas. At the same moment, the girls heard footsteps behind them. They were trapped!

CHAPTER VIII

A Ghost Is Fooled

WITH the ghostly shape swaying toward the Danas and their escape cut off from behind, the sisters' only thought was to get out of Mozart Hall. They ran up the pitch-dark aisle of the opera house. Louise was in the lead, Jean in back.

Suddenly the older girl fell flat against an object blocking their path. Jean, trying to avoid falling on her sister, swerved, but tumbled, hitting her head hard on an aisle seat.

Both girls blacked out!

When Louise and Jean revived, they were still lying on the floor of the theater. The place was in total darkness and Louise gingerly felt around for the flashlight. It was gone!

"Oh, my head!" Jean moaned. "It hurts."

"Mine aches, too," said Louise, as the girls got to their feet. The obstruction proved to be a wooden statue of a gladiator, which now lay between the seats.

"Someone deliberately placed this dummy in the aisle!" Jean exclaimed.

Shakily the Danas groped their way to the side door. Louise reached into her pocket for the key. It was not there! The girls then tried to open the door, but could not budge it.

"Let's try the main entrance," Jean proposed.

The sisters felt along the wall until they came to the lobby. Once there, they walked cautiously across the marble floor. To their relief, when they pushed the great door, it swung open. Thankfully, they walked out.

"Shall we go over to Mrs. Merrill's?" Louise asked, "and report what happened?"

Jean shook her head. "Not now. Later. I just want to get back to our room and relax."

The fresh air revived the girls and by the time they reached Starhurst they both felt better. They decided to consult the school nurse, nevertheless, about their headaches.

After an examination, she announced, "Your injuries are slight and the headaches will soon disappear. I suggest that you have dinner here and get to bed early."

Mrs. Crandall visited the Danas. Jean and Louise told her of their adventure. They purposely omitted the part about the ghost because they felt that the headmistress might think they had imagined the whole thing.

"You must promise me that you will not go into Mozart Hall alone any more," Mrs. Crandall said. Louise and Jean readily agreed, glad that she had not insisted they stay away altogether.

As soon as Evelyn Starr heard that the Danas were confined to their suite she dashed in to see them. "I'm so sorry," she said. "What happened?"

The sisters related their experience. At once Evelyn went to find Fritzi Brunner, but learned that this was the maid's afternoon and evening off.

"I'll have to wait till morning," she reported to Louise and Jean.

Before breakfast the following day, Fritzi knocked on the Danas' study door and then entered the room to express her concern over their fall. Evelyn had just told her of their injury. Louise questioned the maid about Toby Grimes, and asked if she had gone into Mozart Hall. A frightened look came over Fritzi's face.

"Oh, I didn't have anything to do with what happened to you!" Fritzi cried out. "Honest!"

She explained that Toby Grimes was a friend of a deceased relative of hers. It was through the caretaker that she had heard of an opening for a temporary position at Starhurst School.

"When I met Toby yesterday," Fritzi continued, "he told me about a letter he wanted me to read. I went to the back of the house, where he took it from a coat in the kitchen. He gave the letter to me and I walked around the other side of the house to the street. I never went into the opera house. You have to believe me!"

Louise and Jean assured her that they did.

"This afternoon let's hear Toby Grimes's side of the story," Louise suggested after Fritzi had left. The caretaker later corroborated what she had told the girls.

When he heard what had happened to the Danas, Toby remarked angrily, "I suppose you're implying that I don't keep good watch of the opera house. Well, I want you to know I do. If you can't look after yourselves in there, stay out. Your stupid ghost story doesn't scare me."

The girls realized that they would gain nothing by questioning Toby Grimes further about the ghost incidents. Either he believed what he was saying, or he was covering up something.

"We borrowed a key and a flashlight from Mrs. Merrill's maid," said Louise. "We'd like to find them and return both to her."

"I've already done that," Toby snapped. "I found 'em on the floor."

Louise and Jean decided then to tell Mrs. Merrill about the whole affair. She was at home. While she listened politely, the former opera star laughed gaily as Jean dramatically described what had happened.

"Now, my dear," Mrs. Merrill finally said,

"surely you don't believe this story yourself. I warned you that Mozart Hall is full of music and ghosts of the past. As for the hammering in the cellar, Toby did tell me some repairs were needed. I presumed that he was attending to them. I'm sorry if you girls fell and hurt yourselves."

The woman paused, looked out the window, then abruptly summoned the maid and asked to have tea served. Mrs. Merrill began to talk about various operatic roles she had sung. The Danas felt she had changed the subject to avoid further questions.

Louise and Jean were more nonplussed than ever by the woman's blithe attitude. All the peculiar goings-on in the theater were not figments of their imagination. It was not until the retired singer and her guests were sipping tea and munching cookies that she got back to the subject of Mozart Hall.

"Only an hour ago," she said, "I received word that the opera company will rent my building. Unfortunately, they have chosen the very night of the Starhurst musical to begin their run. I'm very sorry. Will you please relay the message to Mrs. Crandall?"

The Danas, stunned by this news, could barely murmur a response. They had felt so sure that Mrs. Merrill was not going to hear from the company. This ruined all their well-laid plans! Where

were they going to find room for all the people
who had bought tickets?

"It's probably just as well," Mrs. Merrill bub-
bled on. "Now you Starhurst girls won't be
troubled by thinking you see ghosts!"

Louise and Jean, trying not to show their concern, laughed politely. A few minutes later, however, they set down their teacups and rose to leave.
Their hostess waved them off cheerily from the
front door.

"This is terrible," said Louise, as the sisters
walked back to school.

They went at once to tell Mrs. Crandall of
the unfortunate turn of events. She was as dis-
tressed as they, wondering what to tell the many
parents and friends who had made plans to attend
Spring Is Here.

Jean had a sudden idea. "Why not push up the
date of the show?" she asked hopefully. "I'm sure
the girls could get ready in time."

"I presume the opera company will want to
move in at least a week before their first performance," the headmistress replied. Then she
smiled. "But I suppose it won't hurt to ask."

Mrs. Crandall consulted the various teachers
who were helping with the musical. All felt that
it would be possible to have the show in shape
several days sooner. If Mrs. Merrill would agree
to let them have the opera house for that time, the

only problem left was to notify the ticket holders.

At nine thirty the students were called to the lounge. Mrs. Crandall announced that she had arranged with Mrs. Merrill to have the musical on a Saturday evening, one week earlier than originally planned. This brought cheers of delight from the girls. The headmistress raised her hand for silence.

"This means everyone will, of course, have to work doubly hard to get ready," she said. "But I have a word of caution. Preparations for *Spring Is Here* are in no way to interfere with studies. Final exams will be coming up soon after the show is over."

The next day a cleanup committee was formed among the students. Using a new diagram Louise had made of the opera house, groups were assigned to the various sections. Work was to start that very afternoon, and all the girls were excused from regular athletic activities.

Mrs. Merrill had arranged for the power to be turned on. Just before Louise and Jean reached Mozart Hall, Doris ran up. She had appointed herself chairman of a committee to gather reports from any students who had heard the Danas' song on the radio.

She sighed. "Up to now," she told the sisters, "not a single student has."

"It's my private opinion," said Doris, "that

Lettie and Ina heard something similar and are just making trouble so Lettie's song will win."

"I hope we can prove she's wrong," said Louise. "The way things stand makes it look bad for us."

As she and Jean led the way into Mozart Hall, Lettie and Ina caught up with the group. When they were assigned the task of dusting off certain rows of seats, Lettie scowled.

"And since when do I have to take orders from the Danas?" she grumbled.

The unpleasant girl announced that she would work exactly where she wanted to and that was upstairs. Furthermore, Ina would go with her. She ended her declaration by announcing loudly, "This whole thing is ridiculous."

The other students heaved sighs but refrained from making any comments. They were used to Lettie's tirades and paid no attention to her. Instead every other classmate willingly began her assignments.

A few minutes later Jean said to Louise, "I have an idea Lettie's up to some trick. Let's follow and see what's going on."

Quietly the Danas climbed the stairs. When they reached the third gallery, the girls heard voices and peered inside. From a bag containing cleaning rags, Lettie pulled out a sheet.

"Now when I walk down and start to moan, Ina, you flash your light on me," she ordered.

"But what'll happen to us if we get caught?" Ina asked nervously.

"You'll be assigned double duty," cried Jean, rushing forward. "If you think you can play while the rest of us work, you're mistaken!"

Lettie, caught completely off guard, was shaken. For once, she was speechless. Dropping the sheet, she blurted, "Come on, Ina."

Both girls fled down the stairs and outdoors.

"I guess we won't miss them," said Louise.

That evening after dinner Evelyn came to the Danas' study. Closing the door, she burst out laughing.

"Tonight we get our revenge," she said and told them about the telegram she had sent Lettie and Ina, signed "The Brothers."

"The girls are all dressed up. Hide near the lounge and watch the fun!" Evelyn would not say any more.

A few minutes before eight o'clock, classmates were hidden at several vantage points from which they could look into the lounge.

Lettie and Ina soon entered the room and carefully seated themselves. A few moments later a maid answered a ring at the front door.

Twin boys, ten years old, stepped into the reception hall. One of them said in a loud, clear voice, "We'd like to see Miss Briggs and Miss Mason!"

CHAPTER IX

Radio Clue

"WHAT are your names?" asked the maid who had admitted the two little boys into the school hallway.

"Jack and James Starr."

"Miss Briggs and Miss Mason are in the lounge. Will you please follow me?"

Meanwhile, Louise, Jean, and their friends were finding it hard not to laugh and give away their presence. Doris stifled a giggle and Ann swallowed hard.

"The twins are cute," Ann whispered to Evelyn. "Are they relatives of yours?"

"Yes, they're cousins. And I must say the kids are dressed for the occasion!"

Lettie and Ina were wearing their most ingratiating smiles as the boys walked toward the lounge. The Danas and the others quickly moved as far forward as they dared. By this time the two roommates were staring dumfounded at the twins, who now sat down opposite them.

"Good evening," said one of the boys. "I'm Jack Starr. This is my brother James."

Lettie and Ina continued to stare uncomprehendingly, not saying a word. James smiled and explained that he and Jack had come to ask a very special favor of the girls.

Lettie, her curiosity aroused, said, "Tell us quickly what it is. We are expecting important company."

In her hiding place, Jean Dana clapped both hands to her mouth and rocked with laughter. Louise gave her a soft, warning "Sh!"

"We heard," Jack Starr was saying, "that you girls are wonderful dancers."

"Yes, of course, we are," Lettie admitted smugly. "But hurry up. What's your request?"

The two little boys looked at each other, then finally Jack said, "We came to invite you both to go with us to our dancing-school party."

For several seconds Lettie was speechless, then she said slowly, "We—would—go—with you?"

The next instant her face grew livid with rage. She bounded out of her chair, leaped across the room, and shook her finger violently at the boys. "Do you mean," she screamed, "that you're the brothers who—— Oh, I've never been so insulted in my life! The nerve of you!" she raved on.

"We came to invite you to our dancing-school party,"
one little boy said.

"Who do you think you are? Who put you up to this? Why, you crazy kids! I'll—— I'll——" she sputtered helplessly.

The twins rose and began to laugh. Jack said, "Sure someone put us up to this. But you'll never find out from us who it was."

From the expression on Lettie's face, the Danas were sure she was going to shake both boys.

"We'd better go to the rescue," Jean said, giggling.

But at this point Lettie had evidently had enough and she flounced out of the lounge. Ina, who had remained silent the whole time, followed.

Louise, Jean, and their friends once more darted into hiding. But as Lettie and Ina started up the stairway, the group could no longer refrain from laughing. Lettie spun around and shrieked. Ina burst into tears. The two hurried out of sight as fast as they could.

"Serves them right," said Ann when the girls emerged from their hiding places. "Evelyn, your brainstorm was a great success!"

Evelyn declared that Lettie and Ina's discomfort was compensation for the trick that had been pulled on Louise and Jean. The girls gathered around Jack and James, congratulating them on their excellent performance.

"And now do we get the ice cream and cake you promised us?" Jack asked eagerly.

"You sure do," said Evelyn.

She disappeared into the kitchen and presently returned with a tray on which were two dishes heaped with chocolate and vanilla ice cream and large slices of angel cake. When the boys finished eating, their older brother arrived to take them home.

"We can never thank you enough for helping me play the trick," said Evelyn. "The joke went off perfectly."

"I'm glad," said Jack. "When James and I heard what happened to the Dana girls, we wanted to help you get even."

The students returned to their rooms. They wondered if Lettie and Ina would make any attempt to speak to the Danas, but they did not appear again that evening.

The following morning Jean turned on the radio while she was dressing. She hummed the various songs that were played. Suddenly she stopped short. "Louise!" she cried. "Listen to this!"

Louise dashed to her sister's side. "That's it!" she exclaimed.

There was no question but that the song being played was the Danas'!

As Ina had reported, the words were different, but the melody was the same. At the end the announcer said, "You have been listening to 'Love Is So Strange.' "

The Danas did not hear any more. They stared

at each other in disbelief. It was true! The melody of their song and the general idea of the lyrics had been stolen.

Jean rushed to the phone and called the radio station. When the operator answered, Jean asked to be connected with the general manager.

The operator said that he was not in yet and his appointment schedule for the day was booked solid.

Jean stated her reason for calling and the woman said, "The best advice I can give you is to write a letter about what you have told me. Send it to Mr. Boyle Smith, in care of this station."

"But——" Jean said. Before she could protest further, the connection was broken. Jean repeated the conversation to Louise.

After breakfast the sisters composed a letter to Mr. Smith. They were so engrossed in their work that they did not hear Fritzi come into the room.

Jean, looking up, finally noticed her. "Oh, good morning, Fritzi."

"Good morning," the maid replied. "I-I heard you talking—something about your song being stolen?"

"That's right, Fritzi," Louise answered. "Somebody stole the melody and the idea of the lyrics. We heard it played over the radio this morning."

A look of fright came over Fritzi's face. "Oh, what are you going to do?" she asked quickly. "What'll happen to the person who took it?"

"He'll probably go to jail!" Jean announced.

Fritzi gave a little cry. "You don't think I took your song, do you?" she questioned fearfully. "You once asked me what I knew about it."

"No, we don't think you took it," said Louise.

"But the real thief may go to jail?" the maid repeated.

"Maybe not that bad," said Louise. "But the culprit certainly would have to pay heavy damages."

"Oh, dear," Fritzi murmured as she started to clean their room.

Louise was putting a stamp on the letter when the maid finished and was about to leave.

"I'll mail that for you," Fritzi offered.

"Never mind, thanks," Louise told her. "I'm going downstairs in a few minutes and can do it myself."

But Fritzi insisted, saying the postman would be coming soon with the early morning mail. She would watch for him and see that he collected Louise's letter. Finally, more to humor Fritzi than anything, Louise handed it to her.

"I wonder how soon we'll get an answer," said Jean. "If one doesn't come in a few days, I'm going to call the station again."

When the sisters informed Mrs. Crandall about what had taken place, she said it was incredible. She decided, however, not to do anything until the girls received a reply to their letter.

During the morning, word that the Danas had heard their song and that it had been stolen from them spread like wildfire. This was the only topic of conversation at lunch hour, which was more noisy than usual. Not until Mrs. Crandall rose to make an announcement did the girls quiet down.

The headmistress said that Miss Blanchard, the art director, had scheduled a short meeting of the scenery committee for the musical. She had requested that Louise and Jean also attend. The committee was to meet in the lounge after lunch.

When the students had gathered, Miss Blanchard said she doubted that the pieces of scenery some of the girls had painted for *Spring Is Here* would be large enough for the Mozart Hall stage.

"I believe we should go to the opera house and take some measurements," the slender, vivacious woman suggested. She smiled. "Louise and Jean, we'll need you with us, since you are more familiar with the place than anyone else." The sisters said they would be glad to go along.

That afternoon, when Miss Blanchard and the girls entered the dark building and beamed their flashlights around, the students' loud, gay conversation quickly changed to whispers. Most of the girls had never been inside Mozart Hall. Louise and Jean, who had grown accustomed to the awesomeness of the old theater, smiled.

"This place won't bite you," Jean assured them,

laughing. "Sure, it has a ghost, but a harmless one!"

Her statement eased the apprehension the others had felt, and they hurried down one of the aisles toward the stage. Louise and Jean were in the lead.

The dark-red plush curtains were parted at the proscenium as usual. But a canvas curtain a short distance behind the red curtains had been unrolled partway down. Louise, noting this, mentioned it to Jean.

"Toby Grimes might have been testing it," her sister remarked.

The words were hardly out of her mouth when, with a thunderous crash, the bottom of the canvas curtain hit the stage. The students jumped.

The next moment they heard a moan from somewhere on stage!

CHAPTER X

The Secret Stairway

"Oh, somebody's been crushed under the curtain!" cried Doris. "That horrible moan!"

Louise was the first to rush up onto the stage. The other girls followed. To their complete astonishment, no one was lying on the floor, either in back of the curtain or underneath it. Was it possible that anyone could have crawled or walked away so quickly if badly hurt? The girls looked in both wings, but they could find no one.

"It must have been the ghost again," Doris said shakily.

Louise remarked that the strange happenings in Mozart Hall had begun to make everyone feel that there really were ghosts. "We'd better shake off this mood," she advised, "or we won't accomplish a thing."

All this time Miss Blanchard had not said a word. Since the unnerving incident, she had looked worried. But finally she asked the Danas if they could explain what had happened.

"I have a theory," Jean spoke up. "I think some honest-to-goodness live person is playing ghost in this old place to scare us off. He even uses various sound effects!"

"Such as?" Miss Blanchard asked.

Jean said that she believed all of the odd noises might be on records.

"Then there ought to be a record player around here," the art director suggested.

The girls searched the stage and wings thoroughly, but could not find one.

"I guess the ghost took it with him," Jean concluded half-jokingly.

For some time, Miss Blanchard looked around the old theater. She observed the heavy crystal chandelier hanging from the ceiling of the auditorium, then the fly galleries, the sandbags, and the other equipment on the stage.

Finally she remarked, "If this—er—ghost should decide to pull any of his tricks during the actual performance of *Spring Is Here*, it might prove disastrous to one or more persons."

Louise suggested that on the night of the performance guards be stationed at vantage points around the building to prevent any such occurrence. Jean said perhaps Ken, Chris, and some other boys from Walton Academy could keep watch.

"We can take care of that later," Miss Blanchard advised. "Right now we'd better check measurements and decide about scenery."

The group spent about twenty minutes on that chore. It turned out that most of the sets they had already painted could be used. Miss Blanchard suggested that they fill in with pieces belonging to the opera house.

"The scenery is stored in the basement," Jean said.

She and Louise led the others to the properties room. The girls who had not seen it before were intrigued. They ohed and ahed about the variety of costumes and masks. On impulse Dorothy climbed inside one of the suits of armor.

"A ghost in armor!" Jean chuckled, as Dorothy stalked stiffly across the floor.

While Miss Blanchard looked over pieces of scenery and most of the group inspected the costumes, Louise and Jean toured the basement. They made a plan showing where guards should be stationed.

"We'll certainly need one at the foot of each stairway," said Louise.

"What a shame!" Jean replied. "That means the boys who are down here won't see the show."

"Maybe we could lock two of the doors and just leave the stairway from the basement to the stage open," Louise suggested. "It can be watched from the top."

"That's a good idea," Jean agreed. "Let's go upstairs and decide where to post other guards."

The sisters informed Miss Blanchard of their intention and went to the auditorium. They felt there should be one guard at each side corridor and another in the lobby. The girls then mounted the stairs to the first and second balconies, and decided on four more spots.

"Now the ghost gallery," said Jean, as the two returned to the lobby. From there, they went up the special stairway to the third floor.

"Two guards for this gallery ought to be enough," Louise decided after walking down one side, across the back, and down the opposite aisle. "One at each corner."

Jean nodded, then gazing upward said, "I wonder if there are more than three floors in this building."

"If there is another one above us, how would you reach it?" Louise pointed out.

"Let's examine the corridor walls more carefully," Jean suggested.

"You mean there might be a secret entrance to the attic?" her sister asked.

"I wouldn't be surprised." Jean smiled. "This place is full of unexpected adventures."

Flashing their lights as they went along, the two girls examined every inch of the wooden paneling. They had finished going over one side wall of the corridor and were halfway down the next when

Jean suddenly cried, "Here it is! Louise, our hunch paid off!"

Jean was pressing on a delicately carved rosebud in the ornate molding. As they watched, a good-sized section of the wooden wall slid open. Behind it was a narrow circular stairway!

"Good for you!" said Louise.

"I'll bet this is where the ghost hides out when he's around!" Jean said enthusiastically.

Quickly the sisters went up the stairs. The area was pitch black and full of cobwebs and dust. Presently they found themselves in a small windowless room.

"Now what in the world was this used for?" Jean asked, as the beam of her light revealed that the room was empty.

"Look!" Jean exclaimed. "There's a grille in the floor.

She leaned over and dusted it off a little. As Louise and Jean looked through the concave grating, they could see flashlights bobbing about far below on the stage.

Jean chuckled. "I guess from up here a person could get a bird's-eye view of the whole auditorium."

As the sisters watched the group onstage, both were suddenly struck by an amazing fact.

Although they were a long distance from the stage, every bit of conversation on it was audible to them!

"I wonder if they can hear us on the stage as well as we can hear them," said Louise.

"Let's find out," Jean proposed.

The girls waited for an opportune moment. They listened as Miss Blanchard talked about some needed scenery for their show. "I did notice something in the basement that could be assembled to make a good facsimile of what I have in mind."

Louise peered through the grating in the floor and said, "I'm sure Mrs. Merrill will lend it to us."

"Oh, Louise, you're back," said Miss Blanchard, looking around. "Yes, I——" Suddenly she realized that Louise was nowhere in sight. "Where are you?" she asked, puzzled.

The Danas were enjoying their little joke. They kept perfectly still. Miss Blanchard and the students searched the stage area.

When the sisters did not appear, Evelyn called, "Where are you two hide-and-seek players?"

"Under the roof!" Louise replied, chuckling.

"What are you talking about?" Evelyn asked, glancing dubiously upward.

"We really are under the roof," Jean insisted. "Fly up and join us—it's very cozy up here!"

Evelyn and the others insisted that the sisters must be nearby and trying to play a joke on them. Someone suggested they might have taken lessons from a ventriloquist.

"Where are you?" Evelyn called out.

"We're not fooling," Louise said. "We'll be

right down and explain everything to you. Meet you in the properties room, girls!"

As Miss Blanchard and the students left the stage, Louise and Jean walked carefully down the circular attic stairway.

Louise was in the lead and suddenly cried out, "Jean, the sliding panel is closed!"

"What of it?" Jean asked. "We can open it again."

But when Louise tried to push the panel aside, it did not move. Both girls tugged, but it seemed to be cemented to the wall.

"We're locked in!" Louise exclaimed.

"Well, I'll sing out to the others," said Jean, unconcerned. "They'll open the panel from the other side and let us out in a jiffy."

She climbed the winding steps once more and called loudly through the grating, then sat back. Any second now Jean expected lights and figures to appear on the stage. But minutes went by and no one came up from the basement.

She called down to Louise. "No luck, but I'll keep shouting. They'll be sure to hear me."

Down in the properties room, the Starhurst art director and her committee were talking to Toby Grimes. The caretaker had appeared suddenly and asked what they were doing. Miss Blanchard explained that they were looking for Louis XIV scenery.

"No sense wasting your time," the man said curtly. "The stuff's no good. It's faded and the audience couldn't tell what it's supposed to be!" Giving them all a dour look, he added, "And now I'll be much obliged to you if you'll leave. I want to close up this place."

"We're not quite ready to go," Miss Blanchard said politely. "If you'll let us have a little more time we can determine whether the theater scenery is usable enough to borrow. We must decide how many new pieces will have to be painted."

"Look around a few more minutes, but I'm telling you it ain't worth the canvas it's on!" Toby explained.

The group resumed inspection. But not long afterward the caretaker announced gruffly that he wanted to go home and get his supper.

"You'll have to leave right away," he said. "I'll open the side door for you."

"All right," said Miss Blanchard, motioning the others to follow her out. Then she whirled around. "Oh, I almost forgot about Jean and Louise. We have to find them first!"

"They're around some place," Toby said impatiently. "I'll look for 'em and tell 'em to meet you on the street near the side exit."

Realizing that it would be useless to argue with the caretaker, the group decided to leave. Miss Blanchard and the students waited on the sidewalk for over ten minutes. By this time they were thoroughly alarmed. What had happened to Louise and Jean?

"If they did find a secret room, they would never have left without showing it to us," said Evelyn.

"You're right," the art director agreed. "And Mr. Grimes probably is at Mrs. Merrill's by now. I'm going over to ask him what he found out. You girls wait here!"

When Miss Blanchard rang the bell, Toby Grimes opened the front door.

"What did you learn? Where are the girls?" the teacher asked.

"Now don't get all het up," the caretaker advised. "I went all through the opera house from top to bottom and called, but the Danas didn't answer. That means they left for sure."

Miss Blanchard did not agree. "The girls might have had an accident in that old building," she said. "I think I'd better look for them."

"Now listen, lady, it ain't likely both of them would've had an accident," Toby argued stubbornly. "I tell you those girls just ain't in Mozart Hall. They must've gone back to school."

His words reassured Miss Blanchard to some extent. Returning to the students, she reported what the caretaker had said. They agreed he was probably right, although Louise and Jean were usually not so thoughtless toward the faculty.

When they reached Starhurst, Miss Blanchard and the others discovered that the Danas had not returned. The art director and Evelyn Starr reported the afternoon's happenings to Mrs. Crandall.

"We must do something at once," the teacher said. "I feel responsible. I-I never should have left Mozart Hall without finding the Danas."

The headmistress looked at her sternly. "I quite agree with you. But that will not help us out of the present predicament. After dinner Professor Crandall will accompany us to the opera house. Evelyn, you know the building well. Will you please act as our guide?"

"Oh, I'll do everything possible to find Louise and Jean!" Evelyn promised.

Her heart was thumping with fear. Had the ghost in the gallery played more than an innocent trick on the Danas?

CHAPTER XI

A Puzzling Rescue

As the anxious group from Starhurst School hurried along the street toward the opera house, a thought suddenly occurred to Mrs. Crandall. They did not have a key to the building!

"We'll ask Mrs. Merrill to let us in," the headmistress said. "As a matter of fact, she should be informed of what has happened."

At the Merrill home the callers were surprised to learn from her maid that the former opera star had already retired. When Mrs. Crandall stressed the urgency of their call, the maid promised to tell her mistress at once.

The waiting group became impatient as minute after minute passed. Would Mrs. Merrill refuse to come down or lend them a key?

Five minutes later Mrs. Merrill appeared. She was beautifully dressed, and the girls noticed that she had carefully applied make-up. This apparently accounted for the delay. Her manner was serene and she did not seem ruffled by the idea that the Danas might need help.

Smiling, Mrs. Merrill said, "I'm sorry more trouble has arisen in connection with Mozart Hall. I understand from my maid that you think the Dana sisters are locked inside." The woman paused and shook her head. "This would be impossible. As for anything having happened to the girls, Toby Grimes told me he had searched the place thoroughly. No one was around."

"Then where have Louise and Jean disappeared to?" Evelyn demanded.

Mrs. Merrill had a theory. "Perhaps they left the opera house and went somewhere else—to a movie, or out on a date."

Mrs. Crandall disagreed instantly. She was positive that the Danas would never do such a thing. "The girls must be in Mozart Hall and some accident has befallen them," she stated.

The opera singer shrugged, still not convinced that there was any basis for concern.

"But I'll get the key," she said. "And we'll go next door at once, since you insist."

Leading the way, the owner opened the front door of the old opera house. "Where shall we search first?" she asked, as everyone turned on a flashlight.

"How does one get to the attic of this place?" Evelyn wanted to know.

Mrs. Merrill looked puzzled. "Attic?" she repeated. "There's no attic in this building."

Evelyn and Miss Blanchard now told of distinctly hearing the Danas' voices from some place in Mozart Hall that afternoon. "We couldn't tell where Louise and Jean were hiding," the art teacher said. "But they both told us of being in an attic over the stage."

The former singer gave a wry smile. "Just a school girl's prank, I'm sure," she commented.

Regretfully Evelyn recalled that they too had thought the sisters were joking. Then she said, "If there is an entrance to the attic in this part of the building, it must be from the third gallery. Let's go up there."

The exertion of climbing the long flight of stairs from the lobby made Professor Crandall puff. Absentminded as usual, he had not said a word during the entire time, except to acknowledge an introduction to Mrs. Merrill. But now he joined in the search eagerly and gave it his full attention.

A thorough investigation of the entire third gallery failed to reveal any trace of the missing girls. Moreover, the searchers could find no door that might lead to an attic.

Finally Evelyn began to shout, "Louise! Jean!" Although she called again and again there was no response.

"I believe we should get the police," Mrs. Crandall stated firmly.

"Oh no! Don't do that!" Mrs. Merrill cried.

All eyes turned toward the woman. Why was she so vehemently opposed to calling the police? Did she have something to fear from them?

Mrs. Merrill explained. "As you know," she said, "I plan to rent the opera house. Calling the police might give it a bad name, thereby ruining my chances of renting. Please, let's wait a while longer and try to find the girls ourselves."

The headmistress was not inclined to delay any longer. She reminded Mrs. Merrill that the safety of her students came first.

"Maybe there is one more thing we can do on our own," Evelyn said hopefully. "While we were on the stage this afternoon, we talked with Louise and Jean. Perhaps if we go back there, we can communicate with them again."

Mrs. Merrill looked relieved, but Mrs. Crandall said firmly, "If nothing comes of this, I'm going straight to the police."

When the group reached the stage, Miss Blanchard stood in the exact spot where she had talked with the Danas a few hours before. "Louise!" she called. "Jean!"

To everyone's relief and delight, the Danas answered!

"Thank goodness you've come!" Jean's voice said wearily. "Louise and I are locked in the attic we told you about. When we went down the stairs, the panel entrance had closed. We can't figure out how to open it."

"Are you all right?" Mrs. Crandall asked.

"Yes, we are," Louise replied.

"How do we find you?" Evelyn questioned.

As the Danas gave explicit directions, Mrs. Merrill stared speechlessly. She said that the existence of the attic room, as well as the secret sliding panel and the spiral stairway leading to the top, were a complete surprise.

"Do you think Toby Grimes knew about it?" Evelyn asked her. "A caretaker should."

"Certainly not!" Mrs. Merrill replied. "He would have told me. Anyway, Toby is away overnight, so there's no way to find out until tomorrow."

Finding the sliding panel was not an easy task. None of the searchers was as familiar with sleuthing methods as Louise and Jean were. Nearly half an hour elapsed before the stairway entrance was opened. Professor Crandall was the "detective" who discovered the correct carved rosebud.

Louise and Jean, covered with dust but happy, stepped out and thanked their rescuers. Heaving a sigh, Jean said, "I thought nobody was coming to let us out and we'd die of starvation!"

Louise described how she and Jean had seen the searchers and had heard Toby Grimes call, and later Evelyn. They had replied, but evidently their voices and pounding had not carried through the thick-paneled wall. When they tried making Toby hear them through the grating, he was gone.

"I'm dreadfully sorry about this whole thing," Mrs. Merrill said. Then she gave one of her mysterious smiles. "But then, you girls are used to playing detective and meeting the unexpected."

No one replied to this remark, and quickly they all descended to the lobby. After leaving the building, Mrs. Crandall thanked the owner for her help, and the group went back to Starhurst.

While eating a late supper, the Danas discussed the secret attic room. They felt that probably it was only one of several hideouts of the person who played ghost in Mozart Hall. It might prove to be a means of trapping him!

"I'm sure he's been hiding up there whenever we were on the stage," Louise deduced. "If so, he probably hears every word we say. No wonder he knows just when and how to frighten us."

Jean recommended that they spray some fingerprint powder on the corridor floor near the secret panel and on the moveable part of the wall. In this way they might get both footprints and fingerprints of anyone eavesdropping in the attic room.

"If we do," said Jean, "then we can ask a professional detective to come and lift them."

Excited over this idea, the sisters and several close friends made a trip to Mozart Hall the next day. They went at once to the third gallery. While the Danas were busy sprinkling the telltale powder, the others walked around. Doris turned to look at the stage and screamed in horror.

Suspended from the fly gallery over the center of the stage was a ghostly figure, the usual eerie light playing around it! At Doris's shriek the strange light vanished, leaving the stage in total darkness.

As soon as Doris had gasped out what she had seen, the Danas held a quick conference. They decided that this might be their opportunity to nab the mysterious culprit.

Louise proposed that she, Jean, and Evelyn stay hidden near the secret panel. The other girls were to walk down toward the stage as noisily as possible to give the impression the whole group had left the gallery.

The plan was carried out, although Doris was fearful about getting so close to the spot where the ghost had just appeared. Maybe it was still suspended over the stage! But their flashlights revealed no sign of it.

The girls remained on the stage for nearly fifteen minutes, while the other three lay in wait in the third gallery. But there was no further sign of the apparition.

"The ghost outsmarted us again!" Jean exclaimed.

"But we're not giving up," Louise declared. "I feel sure he'll appear here sooner or later. Let's come down after classes every afternoon and inspect the powder."

The Danas did this for the next three days, but the area where they had sprinkled the telltale powder showed no prints.

"Maybe we'd better concentrate on our song instead," Louise remarked.

For days the sisters had been hoping for a letter from the radio station. Louise finally decided to telephone Mr. Boyle Smith. The man's secretary answered.

After Louise explained why she was calling, the young woman said, "I'm sorry, Miss Dana, but no letter was ever received from you. I suggest that you write Mr. Smith again."

Stunned by this announcement, Louise hung up. Why had her letter never been received?

"What could have happened?" Jean asked.

Suddenly the sisters recalled that it was Fritzi Brunner who had promised to mail the letter. Had the maid absent-mindedly forgotten to do so, or had she lost it and been afraid to tell them? Or was it possible that she had deliberately destroyed the letter? And if so, why?

CHAPTER XII

The Warning

FRITZI Brunner again! How often the maid had figured in the Danas' lives recently!

Jean went to search for Fritzi. She found her cleaning a linen closet.

"Fritzi, do you recall that letter you promised to mail for us?"

"Letter?" the maid repeated blankly.

Jean patiently explained. Fritzi's face brightened. "Oh yes. I remember now. Why, I gave it to a man who came here."

"But you promised to give it to the mailman," Jean reminded her.

Fritzi giggled. "What difference does it make? This man said he was going right downtown and would mail it at the post office. I thought it would go faster that way."

With a groan Jean told the maid that the letter had never reached its destination. "That man must have lost it or forgotten to mail it. Who was he, anyhow?"

"Oh—uh—just a fellow who was delivering a package," Fritzi replied. Then she added, "I'm awful sorry."

Before Jean could question her further, the maid burst into tears and rushed away.

"What an unpredictable person she is!" Jean thought.

Later, when Louise and Jean were passing Lettie's room, they heard Fritzi's voice. "Oh, Miss Lettie," she said, "something awful has happened!"

The Danas slowed down, hoping to hear more, but the conversation became inaudible. The sisters walked on.

A new idea occurred to Louise. "Do you suppose, Jean," she said, "that Lettie and Fritzi are in league, playing these tricks on us?"

"I wouldn't put it past Lettie," Jean answered. "But Fritzi—you mean that she may have had a hand in our song's being stolen?"

Louise shrugged. "It's another angle in the mystery to work on," she commented.

After breakfast the sisters talked over this possibility and decided to question every Starhurst girl. Perhaps one of the students who had taken part in dunking Louise and Jean might break down.

Hopefully the Danas began their questioning. But it became a long, drawn-out task and took most of the day. At intervals the sisters would report to each other. Always it was the same answer—no luck.

Louise and Jean had just about concluded that either the culprits were not going to give themselves away or people who were not Starhurst students had been responsible for the joke. Louise, wondering what their next move should be, was walking slowly past a dormitory when she saw Amy Winant studying in a secluded corner. The girl had not yet been questioned, and she was friendly with Lettie and Ina.

"Hello, Amy," Louise said, sitting beside the girl. "This is a peaceful place to study. I won't stay long."

"Oh, you don't bother me," Amy remarked.

After a brief silence, Louise said, "This spot isn't too far from the pond."

Amy quickly glanced up and gave her a searching look. "Er—no, it isn't," she replied a trifle uneasily, and looked down at her book.

Louise pursued the subject. "Jean and I aren't sore about being dunked in the pond, but we're naturally kind of curious as to who did it. No retaliation intended."

There was no response, but Lettie's friend fingered the pages of her book nervously.

"Amy, were you one of the girls involved in the prank?" Louise questioned.

Amy lowered her eyes. She did not reply at once. Finally she admitted she had been one of the pranksters. "But I didn't actually help throw you into the water," she added quickly.

Amy insisted that she had not expected the joke to be carried so far. She had been led to believe they were only going to give the sisters a good scare.

"I've felt pretty bad about the whole thing since it happened," said Amy, "and I'm glad it's off my mind now."

"Who was the man with you?" Louise asked.

"I don't know," Amy replied, "but I assumed he was a friend of Lettie's."

As Louise rose, she reassured Amy that her information would be kept in the strictest confidence.

Since the Danas could learn nothing further about their stolen song from any of the other students, they decided that their next move should be a visit to the radio station in Townley, about twenty miles away.

"We'll get quicker results going there," Jean said, "instead of writing a second letter."

"Let's do it. I'll go and ask for permission."

While Louise was on her way to Mrs. Crandall's office, a maid stopped her to say she was wanted on the telephone. Ken Scott was calling.

"How's everything?" he asked.

"Oh, fine," Louise replied, adding with a chuckle, "except that Jean and I are having a hard time solving a couple of mysteries."

"Maybe that's because you didn't call on Chris and me to help you," said Ken, laughing.

Louise agreed that no doubt he was right. "In fact," she said, "we might be asking for your assistance very soon!"

"Great!" Ken said. "But, in the meantime, how are chances for a date? Chris thought we could make it a foursome."

"Jean and I would love it if we can get permission," said Louise. "Maybe this is an opportunity to combine sleuthing with dating."

"At your service!" Ken said instantly.

Louise told him of the visit she and Jean wanted to make to the radio station.

"Sounds fine," Ken agreed. "We'll use my car."

Arrangements were made for the trip after Mrs. Crandall had given permission. The next day after classes the four young people set off. Ken, tall, slender, and blond, was at the wheel. Louise sat beside him. Jean and dark-haired Chris were in the rear seat.

The drive to Townley was through beautiful country and at one spot Ken pulled off to the side of the road for a closer look at the lovely valley below. "Let's get out," he suggested.

They walked a short distance, then sat down

on the soft grass, their backs to the road, and began to talk.

"Now tell us more about the mystery of your missing song," Ken begged. He was leaning on one elbow.

The girls needed no further urging and were deep in their narration when suddenly something dropped with a loud thud directly in front of them. Startled, they jumped up.

"A stone with a note tied around it!" Jean cried out.

"Who threw that?" Louise whirled as she asked the question.

The others turned, too, just in time to see a tall, slender man with red hair running down the road. The boys started off in pursuit, but the stranger jumped into a car and sped off. The Danas tried to see the license number, but the car was too far away.

Louise bent down and picked up the stone. She untied the note and read aloud, "Danas, mind your own business! Go back to school at once!"

Ken and Chris returned and read the note. "Looks as if your mystery man is shadowing you girls," Ken remarked.

The Danas smiled, but said the matter was growing more serious. The red-haired stranger must have known where they were going and was trying to stop them.

"Little realizing," said Chris with a grin, "that you girls don't scare easy."

"Exactly," Louise spoke up. "Come on! Let's get to the radio station as soon as possible and talk to Mr. Boyle Smith."

The general manager listened politely to their case. "It is very difficult to prove that a melody has been stolen," he said. "I suggest that you send me a copy of your tune, as well as an affidavit signed by several witnesses, stating that to the best of their knowledge and belief the music was completely original with you. Then I'll look into the matter further."

"Very well. We'll do that," Louise promised.

The rest of the afternoon was spent having fun. The couples stopped at a picturesque restaurant overlooking a shimmering lake and had a delightful time dining and dancing.

On the way home, Louise asked the boys if they would act as guards at the Starhurst musical. They gladly agreed.

"I know that the show will be a big success," said Ken.

Chris added, "I sure hope your song can be performed. I'd like to hear it."

"If it's not used, we'll give you a private performance," Jean promised.

After classes the next day, the Danas rewrote their song for Mr. Smith. Mrs. Crandall, Miss Rosemont, Evelyn, and Doris verified the original-

"A stone with a note around it!" Jean cried out.

ity of "We're All Mysterious." Louise enclosed
the manuscript and affidavit in an envelope addressed to Mr. Smith. She mailed it on the way
to Mozart Hall, where they were to pursue the
ghost mystery.

Evelyn, Doris, and Ann accompanied them as
they looked once more for footprints and fingerprints in the powder around the secret panel. To
everyone's disappointment, no one had stepped
on it.

"I guess we're not going to discover anything
this way," Jean remarked. "Let's go down to the
stage. I'd like to find out how the scenery in the
basement can be hoisted upstairs."

"There must be an opening in the stage floor,"
Louise suggested. "Let's search for it."

When the group reached the platform, they
beamed their flashlights back and forth across the
boards. Presently they discovered a huge section
that could be raised and lowered like a lift.

The girls were intently discussing this angle
when they heard a thud above them. Looking up,
they were horrified to see that a huge sandbag had
hit a piece of scenery. The mammoth section was
toppling directly toward them!

"Run!" cried Jean.

All the girls except Louise managed to scramble
out of its way. The heavy piece of scenery fell to
the stage, pinning her beneath it!

CHAPTER XIII

The Condemned Building

THE echo of the crash had hardly died away before Jean was at her sister's side. Louise lay motionless, her head, shoulders, and one arm extending beyond the piece of scenery that had fallen on her.

"Louise! Louise!" Jean cried fearfully.

She knelt and beamed her light on Louise's face. Relieved to find that her sister was alive, Jean checked Louise's pulse and noticed her labored breathing. The heavy board and canvas would have to be removed at once!

"Girls!" Jean cried. "Come and help me lift this off Louise!"

Her friends rushed from the wings, where they had fled as the scenery fell. With their combined strength it was quickly raised and moved to one side. Jean tried to revive her sister by chafing her wrists, but Louise remained still.

"I think we'd better take her over to Mrs. Merrill's," Jean said finally. "If she doesn't revive soon, we'll call a doctor."

Gently, Jean and Evelyn carried the unconscious girl next door on an improvised stretcher made from a piece of scenery. Mrs. Merrill opened the door at their ring. One look at Louise and she quickly invited them to come in.

The girls hastily told her what had happened. Mrs. Merrill became solicitous and began to reproach herself for having neglected to test the equipment on the stage in Mozart Hall.

"Please, let's talk about that later," Jean begged. "Every minute counts. We must revive Louise."

The girls had laid Louise on a couch in the living room. The former opera star hurried off for smelling salts. In the meantime, Jean loosened the front of Louise's dress and rubbed the back of her neck.

Just as Mrs. Merrill returned to the room, Louise's eyelids flickered open. She looked up in complete bewilderment at the group. She blinked for several seconds before speaking. Then, opening her eyes wide, she said faintly, "Jean, what hit me?"

Her sister explained what had happened, then urged Louise to relax completely for a while. "When you feel better, we'll call a taxi and take you to Starhurst."

"I think we should phone for a doctor," Mrs. Merrill said, but Louise insisted that she would be all right. Though she felt sore and shaken up, she was sure no bones had been broken.

"I'll see the school nurse," she promised the former opera star.

While the girls were waiting for a cab, Doris remarked that she was sure the ghost had been responsible for the accident. A look of annoyance crossed Mrs. Merrill's face. Quickly Evelyn covered up the situation by saying she believed the falling sandbag was a pure accident.

"Of course it was," said Mrs. Merrill. "If there are any ghosts in Mozart Hall, they are just the ghosts of the music and drama that once walked its stage."

The girls exchanged glances but made no comment. Mrs. Merrill then said, "I shall make arrangements at once to have the stage modernized, so that it will be safe," she said. "The old equipment there is not at all dependable."

"That's a splendid idea!" Jean said. "But won't it take a long time to do that? It might not be necessary to make many changes. Only a matter of installing new ropes, sandbags, and hoisting machinery."

"We won't depend on doing it by hand any more," Mrs. Merrill said. "Mozart Hall will be vastly improved!"

Very much excited about her newest idea, the woman talked on and on. Still concerned about Louise, the other girls were glad when they saw the taxi pull up in front of the house. They thanked Mrs. Merrill, and said good-by.

When the group reached Starhurst, Louise kept her promise to consult the school nurse. She in turn decided it would be best to call in a physician. After a complete examination, the doctor said it was his opinion Louise would suffer no ill effects from having been struck by the piece of scenery. Certainly no bones were broken.

"But I insist that you go to bed here in the infirmary and remain for twenty-four hours to recover from the shock," he ordered before leaving. At once the nurse picked up the telephone to notify Mrs. Crandall of the incident.

The headmistress arrived shortly. "This is most unfortunate, girls!" she said to the Danas. Then, after a few moments' thought, she added, "Considering everything that has happened, I believe it might be best to give up the idea of holding our musical in Mozart Hall. Why Louise, you might have been seriously injured!"

Louise told her of Mrs. Merrill's plan, but Mrs. Crandall was not convinced this was enough.

"But what would we do about all the extra tickets we've sold?" Jean cried out.

"We'll have to return the purchasers' money,"

the headmistress replied. "What else can we do?"

"But we were raising money for charity!" Louise exclaimed from her bed. "Oh, Mrs. Crandall, please reconsider. I'm sure that if Mrs. Merrill has the stage equipment made safe everything will be all right."

Suddenly Jean had an idea. "There's a building-inspection department in Penfield, isn't there?" she asked.

"Yes."

"Then Mozart Hall must have passed inspection," said Jean.

The headmistress conceded that this probably was true. She finally promised to give the whole matter more thought and make a final decision the following day.

She did not have to debate the problem long, however. In the morning the headmistress received a note from Mrs. Merrill. She had enclosed a letter stating that the old building had been condemned! It could not be used by anyone!

Jean was summoned to Mrs. Crandall's office and shown the letter. "Perhaps it is just as well," the headmistress said.

A great sigh came from Jean, who felt very bad about the situation. She knew that Mrs. Crandall was just as enthusiastic as the girls about having Starhurst put on a hit show for a large audience and collect a substantial sum for the various

Penfield charities. The longer Jean thought about it, the more she felt that the sudden condemnation of the opera house did not ring true.

"Mrs. Crandall, may I see the letter again?" she requested.

The headmistress passed the note across her desk. There was no question but that it was authentic. The stationery had the building-inspection-department heading printed on it and the letter was signed by Roy Hutton, Assistant Inspector.

With a heavy heart Jean left the office and headed for the infirmary. Word of this latest difficulty soon flashed around the school and disappointment ran high.

"It's a shame," said Louise when Jean showed her the note shortly afterward. "I wonder how Mrs. Merrill feels about it. Now she won't be able to rent the building to the opera company or anyone else."

In a few minutes Jean left the infirmary. Outside she saw Lettie talking to some girls. "I'm glad that Mozart Hall was condemned," Lettie said gleefully.

"Why?" Amy Winant asked her.

Lettie tossed her head in the air and with a smirk replied, "Oh, I have my reasons."

Normally, Jean would have paid no attention to this statement. But there was something in the way

Lettie made the remark that gave Jean cause to be suspicious. Could Lettie have had anything to do with the building's being condemned?

On a hunch Jean decided to trail Lettie during the day and see what she could find out. Late in the afternoon, her sleuthing was rewarded. Walking around a corner, she came upon Lettie talking to Fritzi Brunner. They were in a secluded spot and did not notice Jean.

"Everything worked out beautifully, Fritzi," Lettie remarked, chuckling.

"You mean they won't have the musical there?" the maid asked.

"That's right!" said Lettie.

As the two separated, Lettie's words, "Everything worked out beautifully," rang in Jean's ears. What could Lettie possibly have meant?

"I'm going to ask her," Jean determined.

She waited until Fritzi had gone, then went up to Lettie. "I want to talk to you," she said pleasantly.

"Is that so?" Lettie replied rudely. "Well, Jean Dana, I have no special reason for wanting to talk to you, so save it. I'm in a hurry."

"No, I'm not going to save it," said Jean, her eyes flashing. "I overheard what you were saying to Fritzi just now, and I want to know what you meant."

"Well, of all the nerve!" Lettie shouted. "You

call yourself a detective. You're nothing but an eavesdropper. And you're not going to find out anything from me!"

With that, she pushed Jean out of her way and stalked off. There was nothing Jean could do. As she slowly followed Lettie up the hall, another idea came to her. Maybe Ina Mason would tell her something. Though loyal to Lettie, Ina was not so clever at evading questions.

Jean waited for a chance to catch Ina alone in her bedroom. Knowing that Lettie had a piano lesson, Jean selected that period to knock on Ina's door. The girl called, "Come in!"

"What do you know about Mozart Hall's being condemned?" Jean asked directly.

Ina's reaction was completely different from that of her roommate. Her eyes widened, and at once Ina looked very jittery. She glanced at the door leading to the hall as if she would like to run out and get away from Jean's stare.

"Uh-uh-nothing!" Ina stammered.

Jean pursued the subject, and finally Ina showed signs of wavering. "I can't squeal on Lettie," she said, on the verge of tears.

"You don't have to do that," Jean said. "Just tell me what you know about Mozart Hall's being condemned."

Ina fumbled nervously with a pencil, stalling for time, in the hope that Lettie might return early from her lesson. Finally, realizing she still had a half hour to wait, Ina sighed.

In a low, hardly audible voice, she whispered, "If you want to know why the opera house was condemned, ask Fritzi's boy friend!"

CHAPTER XIV

An Amazing Address

THE Danas returned to their study and discussed this latest clue. Now a boy friend of Fritzi's wanted the old opera house condemned! Was he the one who had been playing ghost? Was he the person who had taken the music the night Louise and Jean had been dunked in the pond?

"There's only one way to get the answer," said Louise. "Come on! Let's talk to Fritzi."

The sisters climbed the stairs to a wing on the third floor, where the maids lived. They knocked on Fritzi's door. To their amazement, it was opened by Mattie, the regular maid.

"Why, Mattie, you're back!" Jean exclaimed.

"Yes, I returned this afternoon."

"We're glad you're here," said Louise. "And where's Fritzi?"

Mattie explained that the temporary maid had

left about an hour before. "And look at the mess in this room!" Mattie complained.

Louise and Jean were disappointed to learn that Fritzi had gone. They asked where she could be found, but Mattie did not know. Jean hurried to the office to find out, but Fritzi had left no forwarding address. The only one on file for her was Toby Grimes's in care of Mrs. Merrill.

"Maybe Fritzi wasn't so dumb as we supposed," Jean thought as she returned to Mattie's room.

Louise had told the maid all that had happened while she had been away from Starhurst. The Danas and their friends had always found Mattie interested in their problems and trusted her implicitly. Now her eyebrows lifted and she said that the girls certainly had become involved in a serious mystery.

"If I hear anything that might help you, I'll let you know," she said.

"Perhaps you can be of assistance right now," Louise said. "Do you mind if we look around here at the things Fritzi left?"

"Not at all," Mattie replied. "It was pretty mean of her not to clean the place, but maybe it will turn out to be a blessing. Perhaps you girls can pick up a clue."

Strewn about were many comic books, movie magazines, and newspapers. Jean raced back to the Danas' study for the clipping they had found in the music-storage room. Then the sisters searched the newspapers thoroughly, hoping to find one with a clipping gone. Presently they were rewarded. The torn paper exactly fitted a hole in one of them!

"So Fritzi did borrow the choir robes!" Louise exclaimed. "Maybe there are more clues here!"

The girls turned to several envelopes in the wastebasket. All were addressed to Fritzi Brunner at Starhurst, but not one of them had a return address.

"These don't help," said Jean.

By now Louise had taken everything out of the basket except some tiny scraps that lay on the bottom. "I guess this is our last chance to find any more clues here," she said, starting to pick up the scraps.

Louise laid them on Mattie's desk, then she and Jean began the tedious task of putting them together. When the torn bits were in place, the sisters stared in utter astonishment.

The letter had been addressed to Mr. Michael Rokker at the state penitentiary!

"A convict!" Mattie cried.

"Maybe not," Louise said on second thought. "He might be a member of the prison staff."

"But what's his connection with Fritzi?" the maid questioned. "Is he her boy friend?"

Louise and Jean were determined to find out.

First of all, they would tell Mrs. Crandall about their latest findings and ask her advice.

After hearing the story, the headmistress said, "It has come to my attention that Lettie Briggs and Ina Mason were unduly friendly with Fritzi. They may be able to help you."

Mrs. Crandall sent for them. In a few minutes the roommates arrived, with Ina looking fearful and Lettie wearing a bored expression.

"Girls," the woman began, "I am giving you a chance to explain certain stories that have been brought to me. I expect my students to be friendly and kind to those who work here, but if they find any employee is mixed up with anything illegal——"

"Why, Mrs. Crandall," Lettie interrupted, "you're not insinuating that I know about anything illegal, are you? If there's any such accusation against me, my father will——"

"I am not accusing you of anything, Lettie," Mrs. Crandall said crisply. "Rather, I am giving you a chance to tell whatever you care to in connection with the mysteries of Starhurst and Mozart Hall."

The telephone rang. When the woman learned it was an important long-distance call, she requested that the girls wait in the outer office. The four students filed outside and Louise closed the door.

No sooner had they sat down when Lettie burst into a tirade. "You'd think we were in a jail instead of a boarding school!" she cried.

"That's not true," Louise said. "This is one of the best schools in the country. Mrs. Crandall is strict, but we have privileges."

"You're a good one to talk," said Lettie. "You're one of her pets! But you don't know everything that's going on around here. One thing I can tell you—the maids in this place are horribly underpaid. If you knew how little Fritzi was getting, you'd be astonished. I was so sorry for her I gave her a few presents, so she'd have enough to live on."

Louise and Jean looked at Lettie in disgust. Ina appeared upset. It was evident that she did not believe her roommate completely.

"I suppose," said Jean icily, "that this was the way you got Fritzi to do special favors for you— like brushing and pressing choir robes?"

Lettie winced but did not reply. She looked at Ina as if to say, "Did you squeal?" Ina informed Lettie that she could keep secrets.

"I think Fritzi has been used as a dupe in connection with the ghost business at Mozart Hall," Louise said. "And probably she was informing someone about what Jean and I were going to do and when we were planning to go to the opera house."

"And it worked the other way around, too,"

Jean added. "Fritzi, out of gratefulness for your presents, Lettie, told you what Louise and I were doing at times. This gave you a chance to play tricks on us."

Lettie said airily, "Maybe so."

At that moment Mrs. Crandall opened the door and the girls returned to her office. As the conversation continued, Lettie told them she had given gifts to Fritzi and had had her do some mending for her. But she knew nothing about the maid's family or friends. As to the mystery of Mozart Hall, Lettie admitted to climbing inside a hinged suit of armor in the basement and giving the girls a scare.

"But I honestly don't know who the real ghost is," she insisted. "If Fritzi had anything to do with it, she never told me. I have no idea where she is now."

As the girls rose to leave, Lettie informed Mrs. Crandall that again she had heard the melody Louise and Jean claimed to be theirs.

"I'm sure," Lettie went on, "that is proof enough the song belongs to someone else. Don't you think, Mrs. Crandall, that it's time to have the fourth winner announced for the contest?"

The headmistress frowned. "The matter will be taken care of when our investigation is at an end," she said.

"Well, I don't think it's fair," Lettie said. "I happen to know that my song was next in line and I think I should be announced as a winner."

Mrs. Crandall's face grew red. "You know no such thing, Lettie. The findings of the music committee have been kept secret. Furthermore, I believe you owe it to Starhurst School to be courteous and modest. Consider this an order. Good morning, girls."

The four filed out. As they walked up the hall, Lettie was silent for a few minutes. But as soon as she was out of earshot of the headmistress's office, she began finding fault again.

Jean gave Louise's arm a little squeeze, then turned to Lettie and said with a smile, "You really ought to be the one solving these mysteries. You know more about them than any of us."

Lettie, taken off guard, beamed. "You bet I do!"

Jean gave her a bigger smile. "Don't be so stingy with your information. Who is Fritzi's boy friend?"

"I don't know his name," Lettie replied before she realized what an admission she was making.

"But you met him that evening you and your friends were in choir robes," Jean pursued the subject.

Lettie realized that she had already said too much and might as well ease her conscience on the matter. The whole thing had started as an innocent bit of fun. She and some of her friends had wanted to play a trick on the Danas and take their music.

Fritzi had overheard them making plans. Later she had suggested the girls ought to have a man with them in case they needed some help.

"Fritzi claimed her boy friend would be glad to do it," Lettie said. "He was the one who took the music."

"Have you any idea what he did with it?" Louise asked.

"Not the least. I presume he tore it up."

"Why did Fritzi's boy friend want Mozart Hall condemned?" Jean questioned.

Lettie was telling nothing more. She became her usual unpleasant self, refused to reply, and went off with Ina.

"Do you know what I think?" said Louise. "Lettie doesn't know as much as she pretends to, and she's actually scared because she became involved in the affair."

Jean giggled. "I think you're right. What do we do next?"

Louise announced that she was going to get in touch with both Toby Grimes and Mr. Hutton, the assistant building inspector of Penfield.

She telephoned Mrs. Merrill's home and learned that Toby had gone away for the weekend. Since it was late Saturday afternoon, there was no answer at Mr. Hutton's office.

On Monday morning the girls asked for permission to take time off from classes to talk to the two men. Mrs. Crandall agreed and excused Jean and Louise from morning studies. They set off at once to find the caretaker. He was sweeping the alleyway between the opera house and Mrs. Merrill's home.

Louise approached him and said pleasantly, "Good morning, Toby. We've come to ask a favor. Fritzi Brunner isn't at Starhurst anymore and we'd like to have her address."

Toby Grimes stared at her. "I don't know what it is," he said gruffly. "In fact, I didn't know she wasn't still at the school."

"Well, at least you can tell us where her boy friend lives," Jean spoke up.

"No, I can't," the caretaker answered. His face reddened, and he set his jaw firmly. "Why don't you two mind your own business?"

"Because——" Jean began. But Louise took hold of her sister's arm in a signal not to say any more. "Never mind," Jean said quickly.

When the sisters reached the street, Jean asked Louise why she had warned her not to pursue the subject.

"Because I strongly suspected Toby would hinder rather than help us solve the mystery. I'm becoming very suspicious of him. I hope that we'll have more luck with Mr. Hutton."

CHAPTER XV

A Confession

MR. Hutton, Penfield's assistant building inspector, was an elderly man. He wore heavy glasses and seemed nervous and overworked. When the Danas entered his office, they wondered if, because of this, he had failed to give Mozart Hall a thorough inspection.

Louise introduced herself and Jean, then told the man what a blow his decision had been to Starhurst. "We had planned to present our musical there, and turn the proceeds over to Penfield charities," she explained. "We've sold many tickets and there's no other auditorium in town large enough to hold the audience we expect."

"I'm sorry to hear that," Mr. Hutton said.

Jean asked the man in what way Mozart Hall seemed to be unsafe. She told him how Starhurst students had been all over the building recently

and their inexperienced eyes, at least, had observed
nothing hazardous.

"Certain floor joists have been attacked by ter-
mites," Mr. Hutton replied. "And in various parts
of the building, there are sections of wall from
which plaster or paneling has fallen."

"I think I know the places you mean," Louise
said. "Jean and I feel that they didn't just fall down
but had been deliberately hacked away. There are
definite signs of axes and chisels having been used
where formerly there were doors or closets."

The assistant building inspector looked amazed.
He rubbed his chin and said, "Hm-mm!"

The Danas, sensing that they were making progress, asked if Mr. Hutton had made his discoveries
on a routine checkup. "Or was it because of a
special investigation?"

"Maybe you girls don't know it," Mr. Hutton
replied, "but a traveling opera company is planning to rent Mozart Hall for a month. They sent
a man to inspect the place, though it had passed
inspection only six months ago."

The sisters exchanged glances. This seemed to
be an odd thing for the company to do. Why
weren't they willing to accept the decision of Penfield's chief building inspector?

"Was the man who came a member of the opera
company itself?" Jean asked quickly.

Mr. Hutton shook his head, replying that the
man—a Mr. Paul Horst—was the building in-

spector in Mayford, according to a business card
he had presented. Suddenly his face reddened.

"Maybe," he said slowly, "Mozart Hall isn't so
bad as Mr. Horst reported. With our chief inspector away, I've been extremely busy and didn't
have time to check thoroughly myself. Since Mr.
Horst was a building inspector, I took him at his
word. He strongly advised me to condemn it."

The Danas were suspicious at once. The whole
procedure did not ring true.

"Mr. Hutton," Louise spoke up, "would you
please do us a big favor?"

The elderly man smiled. "Name it."

Louise asked him if he would go with them to
Mozart Hall and look the place over thoroughly
himself. "If you're still convinced it should be
condemned, we'll have to accept that."

Mr. Hutton accompanied them to the old building. Using a hammer, a level, and a steel tape he
went over every inch of the building with the ex-
ception of the auditorium ceiling. At the end of
his examination, he admitted that he could discern
nothing unsafe about the place.

"Now if I could only get a closer look at the
ceiling and find it safe," he said, "I would cancel
the order condemning the building."

"That's easy," Jean said, and described the secret entrance and the attic room.

The man chuckled. "You girls are amazing," he
remarked, greatly impressed.

The sisters decided not to take a chance on all of them going into the attic. Louise remained in the hallway, holding the panel open. Mr. Hutton and Jean ascended the circular stairway. When they returned in a few minutes, the man's face wore a broad smile.

"I'm pleased to rescind my order," he announced.

Thrilled, the sisters wrung his hand fervently. But presently his face clouded. "I can't understand why Paul Horst claimed the hall was in bad shape. It looks as if the opera company might be trying to get out of their contract to rent by getting someone to have it condemned."

Although they did not voice their thoughts aloud, the Danas felt that the ghost of Mozart Hall might have had something to do with this latest development. They asked for a description of Mr. Horst and learned he had red hair. Was there any significance in the fact that both he and the man who had thrown the rock had red hair?

Mr. Hutton remarked that it was strange there seemed to be no way of opening the secret panel from the inside. On a hunch Jean suddenly returned to the circular stairway and ascended, sliding her feet across each step. As she neared the top, the sliding panel suddenly began to close. Then it opened again.

"I've found the mechanism!" she cried. "The

outer edge of this step pushes down at two points
—one to open the door, the other to close it!"

"So that's how we locked ourselves in," Louise
said with a grin as Jean came down.

"Well, you two are good detectives," Mr. Hutton stated. "I guess folks had completely forgotten
about this room."

He and the Danas went downstairs and out of
the old building. The sisters thanked him for all
his trouble and hurried off. They wanted to tell
Mrs. Crandall as soon as possible that Starhurst
could use the opera house after all.

"Don't you think we ought to find out why
Mr. Horst condemned Mozart Hall?" Jean asked.

"I certainly do," Louise replied. "I'm going to
call his office immediately."

She went into a drugstore and called the Mayford Building Inspection Department. "I'd like to
speak to Mr. Paul Horst, please."

"I guess you have the wrong number," was the
response. "There's no Mr. Horst here."

"Did you ever have anyone by that name working in the building inspection department?" Louise
asked.

The operator said no, and she had been working there for twenty-five years. Louise thanked
her for her help.

Rushing from the booth, she exclaimed to Jean,
"That Mr. Horst was a phony!"

"I'm surprised to hear it," Jean replied. "Am I glad we didn't get talked out of using Mozart Hall!"

Mrs. Crandall was overjoyed to hear the news and congratulated the Danas on their clever sleuthing. The students, too, were delighted to learn that the musical would be held in the opera house after all.

Only the Danas' closest friends knew it was the sisters who had succeeded in getting Mr. Hutton to rescind his order. Not one of the friends would give the slightest hint to Lettie, who suspected Louise and Jean of having a hand in it and tried her best to find out.

"I wonder if Paul Horst could be Fritzi Brunner's boy friend," Jean mused when she and Louise were alone again.

"I'd like to bet," said Louise, "that if he is, his real name isn't Paul Horst."

Jean agreed, adding, "There's another clue we have to follow up—Michael Rokker, who's at the penitentiary."

An opportunity to do so came unexpectedly that evening, when the Danas received a phone call from their Uncle Ned.

"My next trip has been canceled because the *Balaska* will be laid up a couple of weeks. Your Aunt Harriet and I thought we'd drive up to Starhurst tomorrow to see you."

"Hurray!" Jean cried. "It's about time you paid us a visit!"

Louise told her uncle about Michael Rokker and how the name might be a clue to the mystery of their stolen song. "You'll pass the penitentiary on your way here," she said. "Would you mind stopping there and finding out what you can about him?"

Uncle Ned said he would be glad to do this. When the tall, handsome, ruddy-faced man and his shorter, sweet-looking sister arrived the next afternoon, he brought startling news.

"Michael Rokker," the captain said, "served a prison term of several years for robbery. Upon being released, he went to the home of his cousin. There he became ill and died."

"Did you learn anything else?" Louise prompted her uncle as he paused.

"Just the name of his cousin. I don't know what help that'll be, but it was Brunner."

"Brunner!" Louise and Jean cried out together. They stopped short and their visitors stared questioningly.

"You see," Louise explained, "that's the last name of the maid who used to work here. We've thought all along that she must be involved in the mystery."

The sisters related the story of their stolen song in detail. Both of the elder Danas frowned and

Aunt Harriet said she certainly hoped the girls' song could be used in the musical.

"Of course it will," Uncle Ned declared with a hearty laugh. "By the great horned spoon, my nieces will lick this mystery easily!"

Louise and Jean smiled, then brought their aunt and uncle up to date on the strange doings at Mozart Hall. Uncle Ned teasingly asked them how they ever found time to study, with so many mysteries to solve.

"I'd like to investigate this place," he admitted, chuckling, "and see if we can coax your ghost to show up. I'd be willing to tackle him!"

"Let's go right away," Jean suggested.

A short time later the four Danas started on a tour of the opera house, giving special attention to the two places where the ghost had appeared— the third gallery and the fly gallery above the stage. As they started to leave, Captain Dana expressed his disappointment.

"Are you girls really sure you saw an apparition in this place?" he teased, "or were you spinning me a yarn?"

They had just reached the front door. The captain had his hand on the knob to open it. Jean was about to reply, when suddenly all the Danas froze to the spot.

From somewhere in the old opera house came strange, spine-chilling laughter!

CHAPTER XVI

Imprisoned

THE strange laughter that had sent chills up and down the Danas' spines was followed by a coloratura voice singing an aria. It was coming from the stage of Mozart Hall!

Louise, Jean, their aunt, and uncle tiptoed across the lobby and quietly opened the door to the auditorium.

"Mrs. Merrill!" Jean exclaimed softly.

The former opera star stood in the center of the stage in a long, flowing white garment. On the floor around her were lighted tapers.

"So this is your ghost!" Captain Dana said with a quiet chuckle.

"I guess she is," Jean conceded, feeling a pang of disappointment.

Louise was too fascinated by the scene before them to say anything. Mrs. Merrill's voice still had a lovely tone, but now and then it faltered.

"She's really very beautiful," Aunt Harriet remarked, touched. "It's pathetic to think that such a superb voice is waning."

The aria was interspersed with trills of laughter, which doubtless the singer had once been able to render flawlessly. Now, however, the sounds were grating and the Danas winced each time the woman came to those parts.

Presently Mrs. Merrill stopped. Her gaze was directed toward one of the prompter's boxes. She nodded her head, then began the aria again.

"Do you suppose somebody is coaching her?" Jean whispered to her sister.

"Maybe she's only pretending—remembering bygone days," Louise replied.

As Mrs. Merrill stopped again, then started the song for the third time, Louise told Jean she doubted that the woman was the real ghost of Mozart Hall. It would have been impossible for her to climb up onto the fly gallery and suspend herself in midair," she pointed out.

"I guess you're right," Jean agreed. "But I still think it was Mrs. Merrill's singing we heard those other times."

Louise did not agree. She was convinced that the person who had been trying to scare people away had been using a tape recorder.

"One thing I'm sure of," Jean stated, "is that Mrs. Merrill believes she *is* the ghost. That's the reason why she never gets excited when we tell her about the odd things we see here."

"And also," Aunt Harriet spoke up, "she won't admit to anything for fear you girls might laugh at her."

A few minutes later the ex-opera star blew out the candles. The stage was left in complete blackness. The Danas, straining their ears to listen, wondered what the woman was doing. They finally concluded she had probably picked up the taper holders and walked off stage.

"We'd better go and make sure everything is all right," Louise urged.

The girls flicked on their flashlights and all the Danas went down the aisle. There was not a sound from the stage.

"Mrs. Merrill must have eyes like a cat to find her way without a light," Jean whispered.

When the four reached the stage and stabbed the darkness with their lights, there was no sign of Mrs. Merrill. The candles and their holders were also gone.

"I wonder where she went," Louise said. "I didn't hear any doors opening and closing."

"Maybe the woman is still inside somewhere," Captain Dana suggested.

Aunt Harriet frowned. "Actually," she said, "I don't think we should be too prying. After all, as long as she's doing no harm, Mrs. Merrill has a perfect right to come into her own opera house and perform all she likes."

"Of course," Jean said quickly. "But Louise and I are positive that another person, who has no right to be here, is hacking and digging in her building to find something that's hidden."

"It's just possible she knows about that, too," Aunt Harriet suggested.

"Perhaps," Louise thought, "we'd better stop worrying about the opera house and its ghosts, and concentrate on tracking down the thief who stole our song." After spending several delightful hours with their relatives, the girls said good-by to them and went to their study.

A few minutes later there was a knock on their door and Mattie came in. "I found something that might be a clue in your mystery," the woman said.

"Oh, wonderful!" Jean cried.

The sisters watched eagerly as the maid took an envelope from her pocket and handed it to Louise. She explained that it had been under her bed.

"I was going to throw the envelope away," Mattie said, "thinking it was empty, when suddenly I felt something down in one corner."

Louise pulled a little scrap of paper from the envelope. It was crumpled, but she could make out the name Mozart printed on it.

"I guess Fritzi dropped this," said Mattie. "It's not mine. Is it of any use to you?"

Louise and Jean were still staring at the paper. Did it refer to the old opera house in Penfield? In the light of Fritzi's strange behavior such an idea certainly seemed possible.

"This may be of great value, Mattie," Louise replied. "Thank you for bringing it to us."

After the maid had left, the girls continued to study the word Mozart. The printing was wobbly, as if the writer were either old or very nervous. The sisters felt that this ruled out Fritzi. Although she seemed flighty and scatterbrained at times, they did not believe her handwriting would reflect this.

"I'll bet Fritzi received this from someone for a special reason," Jean remarked.

She reminded Louise of the crude map of Mozart Hall that Fritzi had wanted. It seemed certain now that the former maid had more than a passing interest in the old opera house!

"If we could only find out where she is!" Louise sighed. "There are so many things we should be doing to solve the mysteries. But instead, you and I will have to settle down to hard work for the next few days. We have tests coming up in all our subjects, besides several rehearsals for the show."

"You're right!" said Jean. "Let's hit the books."

It proved very difficult for the sisters to keep their minds off the mysteries, but they forced themselves to confine their discussions about them to mealtimes and bedtimes. Late one afternoon, after a busy day of tests, Jean found a note on her desk. It was a message from Miss Rosemont, asking the girls to come to the faculty house at nine o'clock that evening.

"It's strange she made it so late," Louise remarked. "But I suppose that's the only free time she has."

Just before nine o'clock, she and Jean set off to meet the music teacher. There was a full moon and the girls had no trouble making their way across the grounds toward the rear entrance. A hundred feet from the house, the Danas were confronted by two masked figures in long flowing robes. Louise and Jean stood their ground, though their hearts began to beat wildly. Was this another prank of Lettie's? Or something more sinister?

"Back up!" a man's voice ordered. "Don't scream or you'll really be in trouble!"

"You won't get hurt!" said the other figure, also a man. "We just want you to sign this note."

"What note?" Louise asked.

The second figure beamed a flashlight on a printed paper, which he held out for the girls to read:

> *We stole the melody of our song and we're very sorry. We will not make further trouble and will withdraw our song from the competition.*

"We'll never sign that!" Jean cried indignantly.

"It isn't true!" Jean exclaimed.

Each girl wondered if she dared scream for help. They were about to do so when the masked figures clapped hands over the girls' mouths.

One of the men said, "We'll drop them in the well!"

Although the sisters struggled desperately, both were dragged backward and given a strong push. As Louise and Jean plunged downward into the well, a lid slammed shut above them!

Fortunately for the Danas, the well contained no water. They fell side by side on a soggy mass of leaves. Both girls lay dazed and bruised for some moments, the wind knocked out of them. Louise was the first to recover and struggle to a sitting position.

"Jean! Jean!" she cried out. "Are you okay?"

Her sister mumbled an indistinct reply. Louise reached over and gently massaged the girl's forehead and face. Finally Jean said, "I'm-I'm all right now. How about you?"

For answer, Louise got to her feet and declared that outside of a stiffness in one leg she did not feel too bad. She helped Jean to stand up.

"Ouch! My right arm sure took a beating!" the younger girl moaned. But after rubbing it a few moments, she declared that it was not broken or even wrenched. "It's a good thing we didn't fall another few feet," Jean added, "or we'd really be in bad shape."

"We're lucky!" Louise agreed. "Now, how do we get out of here?"

The girls reached upward as far as they could but were unable to touch the top of the well. In the pitch dark there was no way to tell its exact depth, but they were sure it could not be very deep since neither of them had suffered severe injuries.

"Ugh!" Louise exclaimed. "It's so damp and slimy in here. If we don't get out pretty soon, we'll have a chill."

"Who do you suppose those men were?" Jean asked. "We might have been killed!"

"Don't say that!" Louise begged, a shiver going down her spine.

The girls felt around the sides of their circular prison and discovered that the well was stone lined. "Maybe we can climb up," Jean suggested. She attempted to scale one side of the well, while Louise took the opposite wall. But the rocky interior was so slippery with slime and moss that it was difficult to get a firm hold. Time after time the girls' hands slipped, and they fell back onto the bed of leaves.

"Oh, dear!" Jean moaned finally. "I guess we just can't make it."

Both girls yelled for help until they were hoarse. Again they tried to ascend, feeling around frantically for some indentation in the wall. This worked all right for about five feet up. At that point neither one could find any more footholds. The stones at that height seemed to have been cemented together in such a way that they formed a smooth surface. The sisters slid back to the bottom of the well.

"Maybe I can reach the top by standing on your shoulders, Louise," Jean suggested.

Her sister leaned down, and after a little difficulty, Jean managed to do this. Teetering, she slowly stretched one arm up as high as she could.

"I can't reach the lid," Jean said. "We're really trapped!" Carefully she got down from Louise's shoulders. "I guess we'll just have to wait until somebody rescues us. I never knew about this well, did you?" she asked.

"No," Louise admitted. "Those two men must have uprooted a brush or two to uncover the well," Jean surmised.

When nearly an hour had gone by, the girls shouted again. Still there was no response.

"I just can't stand doing nothing to escape," Jean said finally. "Louise, let me get on your shoulders again. Maybe by jumping up I can reach the top."

Both girls realized that this was a hazardous undertaking. One misstep, and Jean might fall and injure herself badly.

"Stick as close as possible to the side of the well," Louise advised her, as Jean once more climbed to her sister's shoulders.

Hugging the side and reaching out with her left hand toward the opposite wall to steady herself, Jean leaped upward, her right hand extended above her head. Joyfully Jean touched the top of the well!

"Oh, Louise," she cried, landing back on her sister's shoulders, "we're going to get out! I'll push the top up! Are you all right? Am I getting too heavy?"

Louise confessed that Jean's weight was digging a little into her shoulders. "But I can stand it a while longer. See if you can possibly push up the well cover."

Doubling up one fist and crooking her arm, Jean gave another upward leap and pushed against the lid with all her strength. It flew open!

Poor Louise could not weather the force of Jean's landing on her shoulders and both girls went down in a heap on the bottom. Luckily again they were not harmed, and once more they began to shout for help.

CHAPTER XVII

Playing Cagey

THIS time the Danas' cries were heard. In a few moments Mrs. Crandall, Evelyn Starr, and Miss Rosemont leaned over the well and beamed their flashlights into its dank interior.

"Girls, are you all right?" Evelyn called.

Louise and Jean assured her that they were and quickly told their story.

"Oh, how frightful!" Evelyn exclaimed. "When you didn't come back for so long and I saw the note, I phoned Miss Rosemont."

"I didn't write it," the teacher said. "The note was a hoax."

Mrs. Crandall set her jaw firmly. "As soon as we get you two out of here, I shall notify the police. This whole incident involving your song has gone far enough!"

Louise requested that outside of their closest friends, no one be told the full story.

"Wouldn't it be better to let others think Jean and I fell in here accidentally?"

"You're right," Mrs. Crandall agreed. "If the men who pushed you in know they're being pursued, it will make it harder for the police to find them. Now we'll get a ladder."

In a few minutes the Danas were free. They asked Evelyn if she had ever known of the well's existence. She said that there had always been bushes at that spot.

"I wonder how those men knew about the well."

Before anyone could reply, two policemen arrived. Lettie edged to the forefront of the group that had gathered. She was determined not to miss a word of what Mrs. Crandall and the Danas might tell the officers.

To Lettie's disappointment, the headmistress asked the others to come to her office. Lettie was loud in finding fault with Mrs. Crandall.

"It's ridiculous she didn't know about the old wellhole," the unpleasant Lettie said over and over to anybody who would listen. "I think it's a shame we're not better protected here."

At that, Ann Freeman walked up to Lettie and angrily shook her by the shoulders. "Lettie," she cried, her eyes flashing, "you're the biggest troublemaker I ever knew. Why don't you leave Starhurst if you don't like it?"

Lettie's audience melted rapidly and she herself walked off, furious. But no one heard her say another word on the subject.

The following morning the Danas received a letter from the radio station. At last they were to receive some information about their song!

" 'The radio version was written by Harry Stemple,' " Jean said, quoting from the letter.

"And it was produced by Top Flight Records, Inc.," added Louise.

The excited sisters rushed to Mrs. Crandall's office. She was as pleased as the girls to have this information on which to work. After classes the headmistress sent for them. "I learned Harry Stemple's address," she said, "and hired a private detective to interview him."

"Oh, thank you!" Louise and Jean cried together, and Louise added, "I wonder what he'll find out."

Miss Rosemont came into the office and was told about the latest turn of events. "I'm so glad you've been able to track down the culprit," she said. "Let's hope you'll find out the remaining details in the next few hours."

"Oh, it may take days," Louise said.

At this, Miss Rosemont looked worried. "That's unfortunate," she said. "You see, the committee has decided that the fourth winner must be announced no later than tomorrow."

A sinking feeling came over Louise and Jean. Were they going to lose out after all?

The sisters excused themselves and left the head-mistress's office. Jean said, "We can't waste time sitting around thinking of our troubles. Let's get some friends and go to Mozart Hall."

"That's a good idea," Louise said. "We can see if work has been started yet on the stage."

The Danas rounded up Evelyn and Doris and set off for the opera house. When they opened the front door, they heard hammering. A group of workmen were busy on the stage. Footlights and overhead lights were turned on. Electricity had been restored to the building!

"You don't need Doris and me," said Evelyn to the Danas. "Mind if we go on downtown?"

"No. Go ahead," Louise said, laughing. "The workmen will protect us from the ghost!"

When the sisters reached the stage, they were amazed to find out how much work had been done. New ropes and sandbags for hoisting and lowering the scenery had been put in place. An electrical panel had been installed at one side of the stage for push-button control of the heavy pieces.

"There's Toby!" Jean said. The caretaker was leaning against a side wall.

The crew foreman turned to the Danas. "Friend of yours?" he asked, nodding toward Toby.

The girls smiled and shook their heads. "Not exactly," Jean murmured.

"Well, if he was," the foreman went on, "I'd

ask you how to get rid of the fellow. Been here every minute since we started work. You'd think we couldn't do a thing right. Every time we make a move, he follows us."

"How annoying!" Louise replied.

The girls moved away a little distance. Now they glanced at each other. Was there some particular significance behind the caretaker's interference? Was he afraid the workmen might find something for which he had been searching?

Louise whispered to Jean, "Shall we speak to him and see if we can learn anything?"

Jean nodded and they walked over to the man.

"You girls better get out of here," Toby said gruffly. "It's dangerous!"

"Dangerous?" Jean repeated.

"That's what I said."

If the caretaker had expected the sisters to be disturbed at his statement, he was disappointed. They made no move to leave.

Louise, feeling that it was useless to try learning anything helpful about Mozart Hall, asked, "Have you obtained Fritzi's address yet?"

Toby gave her a searching look, then said, "Why are you so all-fired anxious to have it?"

"Well," Louise answered, "something was found at the school that we think belongs to Fritzi. We'd like to ask her about it."

The man's eyes began to glisten and his manner became less surly. "Let me have it," he said, "and I'll give it to Fritzi—that is, if I see her," he added quickly.

"Oh no!" Louise said. "It isn't our property, so we couldn't very well give it away. If Fritzi comes to Starhurst, we'll show it to her."

Toby set his jaw. "Have it your own way!"

"Well, I guess we may as well go," Jean said.

Toby Grimes did not see the wink she gave her sister. When the girls reached the lobby, Jean suggested, "Let's run up to the third gallery and see if there are any new prints in that powder."

"First let's pretend we're leaving the building," Louise proposed, "and then see what happens."

She opened the front door and let it close with a bang. Then she and Jean quietly went back across the lobby and up to the hallway of the third gallery. At the entrance to the secret stairway, the girls shone a flashlight on the floor where they had sprinkled the powder.

"Nobody else has been here," Louise stated.

Before leaving, the sisters cautiously opened a door to the seat section and looked down toward the stage. The workmen had just finished packing up their tools, and a moment later left the stage. Toby departed also. Both the footlights and those on the ceiling were extinguished.

"We didn't learn a thing," Jean whispered to her sister. "Let's go!"

The girls had just reached the lobby, when they saw a light through the glass panel of one of the auditorium doors. Peering inside, they were amazed to see that the footlights had been turned on again. In the center of the stage stood a red-haired, slender young man. He was motioning to someone in the wings.

"He isn't one of the workmen," Louise observed.

"No," her sister said slowly. "His red hair reminds me of that man who threw the stone with the warning note. He looks a lot like him."

Although the Danas listened intently, they could not hear what was being said on the stage.

"How maddening!" Louise groaned. "Just when we might be on the verge of discovering something important."

"Let's go to the secret attic room," Jean suggested, "and listen through the ventilator."

Quietly but swiftly the girls raced up the stairs to the third gallery. As Jean held the secret panel open, Louise climbed up the stairway and put her ear to the grillwork.

The red-haired young man was saying, "I don't think the stuff's in here at all. You and Fritzi are nuts!"

From the wings came a muffled reply, "That's a fine way to talk about me and your financy."

Louise smiled at the odd pronunciation of fiancée, but was electrified at the statement. The red-haired man must be Fritzi's boy friend! If possible he should be captured.

She dashed down the attic steps and joined her sister. Louise closed the door, grabbed Jean by the hand, and sped toward the stairs. On the way down she told Jean her suspicions. But by the time they reached the auditorium, the stage was in darkness. The young man and his unknown companion had left!

The girls went out a rear door and raced up the alley to the street. There was no sign of the red-haired young man anywhere.

"Oh dear!" Jean groaned. "We came so close to solving part of the mystery."

Louise said the person to whom the red-haired stranger had been talking might have been Toby Grimes. On this assumption, the two girls rang Mrs. Merrill's bell. Toby answered.

The Danas told what they had seen and heard in the opera house. At first Toby admitted nothing, but finally he revealed that he had been inside the theater with Fritzi Brunner's fiancé.

"Fritzi once lost a ring in Mozart Hall," he said. "Happened when I was showing her around the place a while back. Her gentleman friend and I have been looking for it off and on."

"What is the young man's name?" Jean asked.

Toby's friendly mood changed instantly. Ignoring the query, he said suspiciously, "Where were you girls, anyhow? Hiding around the stage?"

"No."

"Then how did you hear all this you've been

telling me?" Toby demanded. "Where were you?"

The Danas decided it was their turn to be mysterious. "Oh, in a secret place," Jean answered, and refused to give any further details.

It was evident to them that Toby Grimes did not know about the secret room. This might prove very helpful should the girls wish to use it again!

Without even saying good-by, Toby closed the door. The Danas returned to Starhurst.

"One thing I'm sure of," Louise said later, "is that Toby does not trust Fritzi Brunner's boy friend, or he wouldn't have refused to give us his name and address."

"I don't think it matters," Jean replied. "We'll find the red-haired man as soon as we have time to do a little more sleuthing."

The sisters managed to put the mysteries out of their minds that evening. They had a great deal of studying to do and were determined to maintain their good marks. It was a quiet night. For this reason, both girls jumped when the town's fire siren shattered the stillness.

Moments later Evelyn burst into their room. "Mozart Hall!" she cried out. "It's on fire!"

CHAPTER XVIII

The Culprit

As news of the fire in Mozart Hall spread through Starhurst School, students flew to their windows and looked out toward the town of Penfield. In the glare of powerful searchlights, they could see a billowing column of smoke.

"The whole opera house seems to be burning to the ground!" Doris Harland cried, rushing into the Danas' study. "Isn't it dreadful?"

Louise and Jean felt they must do something. The sisters believed that either the ghost or whoever had been searching Mozart Hall was responsible for the fire. The Danas hurried to the first floor, where they met Mrs. Crandall, also very upset. She and Professor Crandall were going to town.

"May we join you?" Louise asked.

"Yes, of course," the headmistress said.

The four hastened to the scene of the fire, where a large crowd had gathered. Policemen were trying to hold back the excited onlookers. An engine was pumping streams of water onto the stage end of Mozart Hall, where the fire was at its worst. A hook and ladder stood nearby, with firemen fighting the blaze at the rear.

"Let's get out of this crowd and watch from behind Mrs. Merrill's house," Jean proposed.

The Crandalls and the Danas hurried to a good vantage point in Mrs. Merrill's backyard, where they could see the fire fighters. Mrs. Merrill rushed over to them. She was greatly disturbed.

"This is terrible!" she cried, half sobbing. "My beloved opera house!"

The others expressed their sympathy. "I'm sure the firemen will soon have the blaze under control," Louise said reassuringly.

"Oh, I hope you're right, my dear," Mrs. Merrill replied. Then, looking intently at the Danas, she asked, "Do you think someone set this fire?"

The girls did not know what to say. The truthful answer was yes. But they feared that this would only alarm the distraught woman still further. Finally Louise, on a sudden inspiration, said that the electricity had been turned on recently. "Some of the wiring may have been defective due to lack of use and caused a short circuit."

Just then, the fire chief emerged from the rear

door of Mozart Hall. Mrs. Merrill rushed toward him. "Oh tell me," she cried, "are your men able to control the blaze?"

"Yes, ma'am, they're making good progress," he replied. "If we don't run into more trouble, we ought to have the blaze out in short order."

Mrs. Merrill heaved a sigh of relief, as did the Danas and the Crandalls.

The chief hurried out to the street but returned in a few moments, holding a notebook. He disappeared inside Mozart Hall once more.

Presently Louise cried, "There's hardly any smoke now!"

The chief emerged and walked up to the group. Smiling, he announced that the flames were completely quenched and that the actual damage, mostly from smoke, had not been great.

"The old opera house will need a thorough cleaning, but the fire itself has been confined to the dressing rooms in the basement. Until repairs are made, this area should be boarded off. In the meantime, the rest of Mozart Hall can be used."

"You mean it would be perfectly safe to hold a performance here?" Mrs. Crandall asked the chief.

"That's my opinion," he replied. "Would you all like to come inside and go over the place?"

The hall was as bright as day with the firemen's glaring searchlights. The tour of inspection reassured Mrs. Merrill and the group from Starhurst

"Do you think someone set the fire?" the owner asked the Dana girls fearfully.

that Mozart Hall had not been greatly damaged.

"Oh, I'm so thankful!" exclaimed Mrs. Merrill, who was again on the verge of tears, this time from relief. "My opera house is still intact!"

The grateful woman offered to have the place cleaned at her own expense and make the necessary repairs. "I promise that it will be ready for the dress rehearsal of *Spring Is Here*."

"That's most kind of you," Mrs. Crandall said. "We appreciate it very much."

The others expressed their thanks also, then set out for Starhurst. There was great joy among the students when they heard that the fire had not gravely damaged Mozart Hall.

The following morning Mrs. Crandall received word from Mrs. Merrill that the fire chief had decided the fire had not been deliberately set. A workman or someone else in the building probably had carelessly dropped a lighted cigarette in one of the dressing rooms.

Upon hearing this, Louise and Jean went to the headmistress's office for further details. Unspoken suspicions they had held about the fire being incendiary were promptly dispelled.

As the girls were leaving Mrs. Crandall's office, the telephone rang. The secretary announced that Mr. Jack and another gentleman were there to see the woman.

"Send them in, please," Mrs. Crandall requested. "Louise and Jean, will you please stay?"

Two young men entered. One was introduced to the girls as Mr. Jack, the detective Mrs. Crandall had engaged. He, in turn, introduced his companion as Mr. Harry Stemple, who appeared to be very nervous.

"These are the Dana girls, whose song was stolen," Mrs. Crandall said.

Hearing this, Harry Stemple winced and spoke in a stammering, almost frightened, manner. "This is what happened," he blurted out. "Some weeks ago I was approached by a man named Horst. He had written a popular song but couldn't see any chance of getting it published because he was not known. Horst came to me, knowing I've had a number of successful songs. Foolishly I let myself be persuaded into making an arrangement with him. And it was such a terrific song I was convinced that it would be a big hit."

Stemple went on to explain that Mr. Horst had given him money to cover certain costs. In return, Stemple was to peddle the tune, calling it his own and sharing royalties with Horst.

"He gave me an idea for some words and I put them into verse." Stemple looked down at the floor. "Believe me when I say that I had no idea Horst had stolen the melody. I hope that you won't bring charges against me. I'll do anything I can to make amends."

The young man's expression was so woebegone that Louise and Jean felt sorry for him. They were convinced that he was completely innocent. At a nod from Jean, Louise said, "If your story is verified, we won't prefer charges."

Jean added, "Will you see that the song is taken off the market at once and an announcement of the plagiarism made?"

"I'll do that," Stemple promised. "I'll explain the whole thing to Top Flight Records." He grimaced. "That won't be pleasant, but I deserve it, I guess. They made only a few test records and sent them to certain disk jockeys in various parts of the country. The radio station over which you heard the tune was one of them."

When Mrs. Crandall asked Stemple where Mr. Horst was, he said he did not know: Mr. Jack verified this bit of information. They were going to continue their hunt for him.

Suddenly Jean had an idea. "Was Mr. Horst's first name Paul and did he have red hair?"

Stemple nodded.

"Then I think he may be found right here in Penfield," Jean said, and told of the Danas' suspicions about him.

"I'll ask the police to help us find him," Mr. Jack announced, then the two men went off.

After their departure, Mrs. Crandall gave the Danas one of her rare, beaming smiles. Then she said, "You don't know how happy it makes me this mystery is beginning to unfold. The judges felt very bad that your outstanding song could not be among the winners."

"We did, too," Jean answered. "But it's all over now!"

"I'll personally take charge of any legal matters in connection with the theft of the song," the headmistress went on. "I hope that it will not be long before Horst is apprehended."

Overjoyed, the Danas thanked her, then hurried off to classes. Soon every student at Starhurst was talking excitedly about the latest findings. Lettie Briggs panicked. It was rumored that she was fearful of being involved in a serious court case, but she did not come to the Danas with either an explanation or an apology.

"Let's try to forget her," Jean said, as she and Louise retired that night. "Even though she has made mountains of trouble for us."

Louise had a faraway look in her eyes. Staring into space, she suddenly remarked, "Jean, I think I know where that mysterious treasure is hidden in Mozart Hall."

CHAPTER XIX

Phantom at Rehearsal

"You've solved the mystery?" Jean exclaimed, looking unbelievingly at her sister.

"I think I may have a very good clue."

"Well," Jean begged, "don't keep me in suspense! Tell me quick!"

Louise opened her desk drawer and took out an envelope. It was the one Jean and Mattie had suspected Fritzi of dropping—the one that bore the printed word Mozart.

The younger Dana girl raised her eyebrows questioningly.

"Jean," said Louise slowly, "when you're in the auditorium of the old opera house and look directly at the stage, what do you see?"

"The frieze, with the large letters spelling out the name Mozart."

Her sister nodded, then stated that she believed

there might be openings behind each letter. "If so, something may be hidden in one of them."

Jean gave her sister a tremendous hug. "You're an absolute genius! I think you have solved the mystery for sure! The sooner we can take a look at the frieze, the better!"

The Danas' hopes for investigating the spot during the next few days did not materialize. Mozart Hall was never empty—carpenters, painters, and cleanup men were busy in every part of the building.

In the evening the opera house was used for rehearsals. Various groups of girls were on the big stage, rehearsing their parts, and the scenery committee was working backstage on the props.

Though the Danas chafed at the delay in investigating the frieze, they kept practicing "We're All Mysterious" over and over.

Dressed as a young couple, in attractive seventeenth-century costumes, the sisters were to sing a duet. Then, quickly slipping off the old-fashioned garments, they would appear in modern dress and repeat their song at a quicker tempo.

As Evelyn watched her friends perform the song, she became increasingly enthusiastic. "It's simply super!" she commented.

The Danas hoped her enthusiasm would be shared by others on the night of the performance.

Before bedtime one evening, Mrs. Crandall

came to the sisters' study. She had just received a phone call from Mr. Jack. Though the detective and Harry Stemple had combed Penfield, they had failed to locate Paul Horst. They had gone to the address he had used and learned that Horst had moved, leaving no forwarding data.

"You don't suppose Horst found what he was looking for and skipped out?" Jean asked.

"Let's hope not!" Louise said.

Finally, the night arrived for the dress rehearsal of *Spring Is Here*. Most of the students were in a nervous flutter and running around excitedly. Some were on the verge of tears, feeling certain they would forget their lines.

"All we need now," Jean said, grinning, "is the appearance of our ghost in the gallery!"

"Sh! Don't even mention the word ghost!" Louise cautioned with a wink.

Shortly afterward, the rehearsal got under way. The colorful settings were charming, and the girls looked strikingly attractive in the Louis XIV costumes.

The first scene went smoothly and no one forgot her lines. As the end of the first act drew near, most of the players came on stage for the chorus, which closed the act. They were starting this number when Doris let out a terrified shriek.

"The ghost!" she exclaimed, shivering with fear and pointing to the third gallery.

The other girls fearfully looked upward. There, a weird white figure was moving slowly, as if through space. Instantly there was pandemonium on the stage.

"The place is haunted!" one girl gasped.

"I won't act in this old opera house for anything in the world!" another burst out.

Louise and Jean realized that unless something was done in a hurry to calm the players the musical would be ruined.

"We must keep the girls from running out!" Jean said. "You guard the door. I'll take this one."

Stationing themselves at the exits, the Danas pleaded with the members of the cast. "Even if there is a ghost," Jean said soothingly, "it never harmed anyone."

"Somebody is probably putting on the whole act just for fun," Louise told them. "Surely you girls are not going to let him have the last laugh!"

"But-but how do you know it's a real person and not a ghost?" one student asked.

"Don't tell me you honestly believe in ghosts," Louise said, half-teasing.

Sheepishly the girl admitted that she did not. "You're right, Louise," she said.

The other students, reassured by the Danas' sensible attitude, resolved that they, too, would not be afraid of make-believe ghosts. At last all the young actresses went back onstage to finish the closing number of the first act. As they walked on, all eyes involuntarily turned to the third gallery. It was in darkness. The ghost, as usual, had vanished shortly after appearing!

Jean hurried over to Miss Rosemont, who praised the Danas for restoring order.

"I'm glad we could help," Jean said modestly. Then she added, "Would you let Louise and me skip this last number and go to the third gallery? The ghost may still be hiding there. He might not suspect that we've left the rehearsal and this may be our chance to corner him unawares."

The music director was reluctant at first to allow the Danas to take such a risk, but when Jean assured her that they would only look and not try to capture the culprit, Miss Rosemont gave her consent. Jean and Louise swiftly went out through the rear, ran down the alleyway, and reentered the opera house by the front door.

In a few minutes the girls reached the third gallery, having negotiated the stairs without using the flashlight Jean carried. It was not completely dark because of the reflection from the stage illumination.

They stood motionless a few moments, listening intently. But the closing music of the first act drowned out any sound the ghost might be making if he were nearby. When the sisters' eyes became accustomed to the dim light, they thoroughly searched the hallway and every row of seats in the third gallery.

"Do you suppose he's up in the secret room?" Jean suggested.

"Now's the time to find out," Louise said.

The girls turned on the flashlight, opened the sliding panel, and shone the light upward. Seeing no one, Jean climbed a few steps until she could look into the floor above. But the ghost was not there.

"Well, he escaped us again," she said in disappointment, as the girls closed the secret panel and returned to the stage.

"No luck," they reported to Miss Rosemont.

The rest of the rehearsal went well and without further disruption. Weary but happy, the players trudged back to the dormitory and went to bed.

Early the following afternoon, parents, relatives, and friends congregated in and around Penfield. They wanted to be in plenty of time for the musical that evening. Among them were Uncle Ned and Aunt Harriet. Louise and Jean, busy with last-minute preparations, were able to spend only a few minutes with them.

"Good luck tonight!" Aunt Harriet said, kissing her nieces good-by. She and her brother planned to have an early dinner in town.

Captain Dana chuckled, saying he expected his

"two me hearties" to put on the best performance of their lives.

Late that afternoon, Louise reminded Jean that they had not yet carried out their intention of examining the frieze in Mozart Hall. "Maybe Mrs. Crandall would let us go down early so we'd have time to look around while no one else is there," she suggested.

"That's a good idea," Jean agreed. "I'll ask."

Obtaining permission, the sisters set off and reached the opera house half an hour before anyone was expected to arrive. Since they had learned how to work the panel board that controlled the stage lights, it was simple to turn them on.

Eager to start their investigation of the frieze, the two girls climbed nimbly up a ladder leading to the fly gallery over the center of the stage and went forward.

When they reached the section behind the giant letters of the word Mozart, Louise proposed that she start with the M and Jean with the T. Leaning far over the railing of the catwalk, they searched hopefully for openings.

"Nothing here but an empty hole." Jean sighed. Louise reported the same for her letter.

The girls inspected the O and the R. Again they had no luck. Louise had just begun on the Z when she gave a cry of delight.

"I've found something!"

Excitedly Jean watched as her sister reached

down. She brought up a handful of shining jewelry! Louise and Jean were speechless. They had found the secret of Mozart Hall!

"Do you suppose these are Mrs. Merrill's stolen heirlooms?" Jean asked.

"From the description she gave us, I'm sure they are," Louise said. "Let's ask her right now."

The girls carefully put the gorgeous necklaces, bracelets, and rings in their pockets. As the sisters crossed the fly gallery quickly and began to descend the ladder, they heard some of the performers arriving. Louise looked at her watch and saw with dismay that there was not time to go to Mrs. Merrill's house now. They were due to have their make-up applied.

"Let's hide the jewelry until after the show," Jean suggested. "But where?"

After a moment's thought, the two girls decided that the prompter's box that was like a little chest would be an ideal spot. The box would not be opened during the performance and directly afterward the Danas would announce their discovery.

As the sisters finished concealing the gems, the first contingent of Starhurst actresses came into the auditorium. In a short while the entire cast assembled. What a flurry there was! One by one the girls were carefully made up for their particular roles. Then, amid much giggling, they helped one another into their costumes.

A wave of excitement swept through the dressing rooms when someone said the audience was starting to arrive.

"Goodness!" Jean exclaimed. "They're early!"

Louise laughed. "They must be expecting a terrific show. We mustn't disappoint them!"

By curtain time the place was filled. Penfield charities would certainly receive a good boost. As prearranged, guards, among whom were Ken Scott and Chris Barton, were placed at vantage points around the building to forestall any tricks on the part of the ghost.

At last the orchestra broke into the overture, and the velvet curtains were drawn back. When the lively strains of music died away, the painted canvas was rolled up for the first act. The opening number brought a storm of applause from the audience.

Halfway through the act, Ann Freeman did a solo dance. It was a toe number and she whirled gracefully through the intricate steps, to the great enjoyment of the onlookers.

Just as she finished, every light in the theater went out. There was a hushed silence for a moment, then a piercing scream!

Instantly the Danas, who were in the wings, recalled the night many years before when Mrs. Merrill had been robbed. Was this to be a repetition of that fateful evening?

CHAPTER XX

Echoing Applause

As the curtain rolled down with a bang, there was an uproar in darkened Mozart Hall. Many on the stage and a few in the audience knew the story of the mysterious theft years before. Would a gun be fired? Might someone be injured?

After the first shock was over, Jean Dana realized that the stage lights must be put back on instantly. She made her way as quickly as possible among the jostling players and found the panel board. One by one she flicked the switches. The place became a blaze of lights.

Louise cried out. A slender red-haired man was taking the jewels out of the prompter's box!

"Stop that!" she ordered, rushing over.

Instantly the man was surrounded by the cast. He tried to escape, but the girls held onto him.

At that moment Toby Grimes ran forward.

Seeing the man and the jewels, he yelled, "You double-crosser! Sid Looper, you're a thief!"

The Danas and the other actresses stared in amazement. Louise demanded an explanation from both men. "But first tell me," she added, "are these Mrs. Merrill's lost jewels?"

Toby replied that they probably were. He asked how they had got into the prompter's box. When Jean told him, the caretaker's eyes bulged in astonishment.

Looper said, "I saw them put the loot there!"

"We intend to turn these jewels over to Mrs. Merrill!" Jean concluded.

Louise now looked toward Toby. Before she could question him, he volunteered, "I'll tell you the whole story. Everything I did was for Mrs. Merrill's sake. That's how come I got myself a job here. I'm not a thief, and if I'd known Looper was, I never would have bothered with him."

The caretaker explained that Fritzi Brunner had been living with an aunt. Her cousin, Michael Rokker, had come to her home after being released from prison. He had become seriously ill and knew he would not live long.

"Michael sent for me," Toby explained. "We were old friends, but I hadn't seen him in a long while. He pulled several robberies. But one the police never learned about was here at Mozart Hall. Mike slipped out of the audience, went onstage and took Mrs. Merrill's jewelry. He hid it in a spot he'd seen while working on stage as a carpenter.

"Mike thought they'd be safe until he could come back for them. But he was caught for the other robberies and missed his chance.

"On his death bed he wanted to make it up to Mrs. Merrill. He was sorry for firing the shot that scared everybody and nearly caused a panic. Mike asked Fritzi and me to get the jewelry and return it. Then, at that point in Michael's story, his throat suddenly became paralyzed and he couldn't tell us the rest. We handed him paper and pencil. He was only able to write the word Mozart. Then he died."

The caretaker said that he and Fritzi had decided, because of the word Mozart, that Mrs. Merrill's jewels must be hidden some place in the opera house.

"Through Mrs. Merrill," he said, "I got a job for Fritzi at Starhurst. In her off time, we hunted and hunted through this place, but we couldn't find the jewels.

"Finally Fritzi suggested that we ask her boy friend, Sid Looper, to help us. He began hacking doors and closets that had been nailed shut or plastered over.

"Right after he started working with us, there was talk of the musical being held here. Sid and

I decided we had to do something to keep you girls out of the place. So we tried scaring you off."

Louise spoke up. "Did both of you then play ghost?"

Sid confessed that they had. "I know a little about magic and I was a ham actor for a while. I showed Toby some tricks."

The caretaker said that they had used a portable tape recorder to produce the various weird sounds and soprano voice the girls heard at times. Sid had been responsible for the sandbag incident.

"It was easy to fool Mrs. Merrill about the ghost business," Sid bragged. "She liked to play mysterious around here once in a while herself. And Toby convinced her that she also walked in her sleep or a trance and played ghost sometimes when she didn't even remember it!"

Suddenly Fritzi Brunner raced into the midst of the group. The girl's eyes were blazing as she made a beeline for Sid. Shaking an angry fist at his face, she cried, "So you call yourself my boy friend. And you even said you wanted to marry me! Well, you never will. I've found out you're wanted by the police!"

"That's not true!" Sid protested. But Fritzi instantly backed up her accusation by motioning to a policeman trying to get through the crowd of girls. Sid Looper wilted when the officer identified him as a wanted criminal.

"Come along!" the policeman said. He snapped handcuffs around Sid's wrists and advised him of his rights.

Louise stepped forward. "Please, officer, I'd like to ask Sid a few questions in connection with another case."

"What else do you want to know?" Sid demanded.

Louise asked, "Did you use the alias Paul Horst?"

"So you found that out, too," Sid growled.

"Yes, we did! And you stole the song my sister and I composed and sold it."

Looper did not deny this and said he was sorry he got Harry Stemple into trouble. "I want everybody to know that Harry is innocent," he said.

"And I'm innocent, too!" Fritzi exclaimed. "I didn't do any harm. But Sid—— I gave him the Danas' letter to mail, and he never did."

Fritzi explained that she had received clothing and jewelry from Lettie Briggs and in return had promised to help play a few tricks on Louise and Jean. Fritzi had secretly borrowed the choir robes and later pressed them and put them away. Lettie had once taken the song from the Danas' room as a joke, but it was Sid who had snatched it just before the sisters were dunked in the pond.

Louise now asked Looper if he had climbed a ladder to the sisters' study and helped himself to a copy of "We're All Mysterious." The man admitted he had.

"Fritzi had heard you singing your catchy tune," he said. "That's why I worked things so I could steal it."

"Why did you take two copies?" Louise asked.

"To keep you from turning the song in until I could get it on the market."

With the whole story told, the policeman was about to take Looper away when, from the wings, Ken Scott and Chris Barton appeared with a prisoner of their own. The boys explained that while guarding one of the first-floor halls from a doorway to the auditorium they had seen the man turn off the dim side lights of the auditorium at a wall panel in the corridor. He ran off, but they turned the lights back on and finally nabbed him.

Suddenly Jean had an idea and shot a question at the newcomer. "Are you the man who helped Sid Looper push my sister and me down the well?"

Hanging his head, he confessed. Evelyn suddenly recognized him as a former gardener on the Starhurst grounds. He admitted having discovered the old wellhole and telling Looper about it. The policeman said he would take both men in.

Just then Mrs. Crandall and Mrs. Merrill arrived backstage. Jean and Louise gathered up the jewelry and presented the exquisite pieces to the former opera star.

"We found these, Mrs. Merrill," Louise said, smiling. "Are they yours?"

The singer gasped. But in a moment she recovered her composure, fingered a necklace lovingly, and said, "You found these in Mozart Hall? It is amazing. You dear, dear girls!"

She listened attentively as the story of the recovery of the jewelry and the girls' stolen song was revealed to her and Mrs. Crandall.

Mrs. Merrill hugged the Danas. "You're the most wonderful girls, and the whole world must know about it!"

Before Louise and Jean realized what she meant, Mrs. Merrill slipped on all her jewelry, then dashed around in front of the curtain and waved for silence in the vast auditorium. In dramatic fashion she told how the Danas had faced danger and unjust accusations to help her and send a wrongdoer to prison.

At the end she insisted that Louise and Jean appear for a bow. The applause was tremendous. The sisters flushed with embarrassment and were glad when they were allowed to return backstage.

The curtain went up again and the second act began. The players, thrilled and excited that at last the two mysteries had been solved, put on an excellent performance. Shortly before the finale the Danas sang their song.

At the musical's conclusion, the applause and

cries of commendation were loud and long. Ken and Chris could be heard above everyone else. Encores were demanded. Louise and Jean did their number three times.

Would they ever be so excited again, they wondered, unaware of the intriguing mystery that lay ahead, *The Curious Coronation*.

When the performance of *Spring Is Here* was over, enthusiastic relatives and friends rushed onto the stage. Through the maze of people, Louise and Jean saw Mrs. Crandall and a strange man coming toward them. Smiling, she introduced him as Mr. Daly, head of a music-publishing concern. To the sisters' utter astonishment, he not only congratulated them on their original song, but also asked for exclusive rights to publish it.

"I believe the song will be a hit," he said.

"Oh, how wonderful! We'll be famous!" Jean laughed.

Louise, still overwhelmed by Mr. Daly's offer, was only able to whisper, "It's too good to be true —and almost as unreal as our ghost in the gallery!"

Mr. Daly smiled and gave the sisters a long look, followed by a chuckle. "And I'd like to know how two girls as young as you have discovered that *we all are a little mysterious?*"